Baseball Coach's Collection of Drills and Games

Improving Individual and Team Performance

Robert G. Hoehn

MacGregor Sports Education
Waukesha, Wisconsin

To my parents, George and Pearl, for their lifelong support
of my educational and athletic pursuits.

Library of Congress Cataloging-in-Publication Data

Hoehn, Robert G.
    Baseball coach's collection of drills and games : improving
individual and team performance / Robert G. Hoehn
        p.   cm.
    ISBN 0-941175-27-8
    1. Baseball—Coaching. I. Title.
GV875.5.H64 1989
796.357'07'7—dc19   88-37683
                                                                        CIP

ISBN   0-941175-27-8

Printed in the United States of America

Contents

How This Book Will Help You and Your Team

Two problems that face most of us as baseball coaches are: (1) what activities to include in practice; (2) how to keep every player busy during practice. *Baseball Coach's Collection of Drills and Games* gives you drills and games for each athlete that stress the skills necessary for successful team play. Each activity includes objective, location, technique, procedure, and comments. This practical guide works hand in hand with you, the coach, by:

- Providing 82 activities that help players improve throughout the season.
- Arousing player interest and motivation through competitive games. Gamelike activities appear throughout the book. For example, Chapter 5, "Drills and Games for the Entire Team," presents thirteen activities that give each athlete a chance to sharpen his hitting, bunting, fielding, throwing, and base-running techniques.
- Permitting athletes to work in small groups.
- Offering fifteen indoor activities, three per chapter, for players to practice during inclement weather.
- Describing game-winning team offensive and defensive strategies (Chapters 4 and 5).
- Including drills and games on how athletes can improve their fielding, throwing, and hitting.

Ten charts and eleven illustrations have been carefully selected to help you prepare your daily practice schedule. Also, equipment that is mentioned in the book is generally inexpensive, easily constructed, and adaptable to any playing field.

Bob Hoehn

chapter one

Drills and Games for Pitchers and Catchers

There are several factors that determine how successful a pitcher will be. These include mental attitude, physical condition, alertness, quickness, and the ability to execute fundamentals. A pitcher, to be effective, must do many stretching, strengthening, and running exercises throughout the season.

The catcher is the heart of the team—the "holler guy." He directs the team's defense and keeps the infield constantly alert. A smart catcher studies every hitter and adjusts his target accordingly. He should be strong, have quick reflexes, and a powerful arm.

The following six small-group drills provide practice for pitchers in strengthening the legs, warming up the pitching arm, keeping the ball low in the strike zone, and coming off the mound.

The popular pick-up drill requires a pitcher to keep his body low and field baseballs tossed to his left and to his right. He fields between 25 and 50 balls before switching with his partner. Copy Cat and Flip-Dip are variations of pick-up.

1 COPY CAT

Objective: To strengthen the legs.
Location: Anywhere on the field.

1

Technique: Athletes practice staying low and moving briskly to the left and to the right.

Procedure: Have athletes do the following—

- Three pitchers form a group.
- The athletes form a straight line. Player 1 positions himself about 25 to 30 feet in front of Player 2. Player 3 stays approximately 6 to 8 feet directly behind Player 2.
- Action begins when Player 1, feeder, tosses a ball to one side of Player 2. Player 2 fields and makes an underhand return to Player 1. Player 3, copy cat, stays behind Player 2 and simulates fielding the ball.
- Play continues as Player 2, running from side to side, fields 25 to 50 balls. Player 2 then becomes Player 3, Player 3 becomes Player 1, and Player 1 becomes Player 2.

Comments: Urge athletes to make an all-out effort. Tell players to use both hands when fielding the ball. SUGGESTION: Have pitchers do 25 pick-ups during the first few days of practice. Gradually increase the number to 50 and 75.

2 FLIP-DIP

Objective: To strengthen the legs.
Location: Anywhere on the field.
Technique: Athletes practice staying low and moving briskly to the left and to the right.

Procedure: Have athletes do the following—

- A pitcher brings a glove and a ball onto the field. He starts play by tossing the ball 15 to 20 feet to one side. After the ball comes to rest, he sprints over and picks it up with both hands. He continues action by tossing the ball to his opposite side.
- The pitcher repeats throwing the ball from side to side 25 to 50 times.

Comments: See Drill 1, Copy Cat.

An early season program should include easy throwing while the pitcher is getting his legs into shape. The following two activities will help a pitcher ready his arm for competition.

3 EASY DOES IT

Objective: To gradually warm up the pitching arm.
Location: Anywhere on the field.
Technique: Athletes practice warming up their arms in a smooth, easy manner.

Procedure: Have athletes do the following—

- Pitchers pair off and stand about 60 feet apart. They take turns pitching and catching balls thrown at half speed. The receiving player gives the hurler a target by holding his glove still. The hurler concentrates on hitting the glove.

Comments: Pitchers gradually add speed to each pitch until they are throwing at three-quarter speed. After a few days, have pitchers pair off with catchers and continue working on their control. SUGGESTION: Caution pitchers to throw only straight balls at first. Throwing too many curve balls early in the season places a heavy strain on the arm muscles. A hurler should increase the number of pitches as his arm becomes stronger. For example, if he throws 30 pitches at first, he should increase the number of pitches to 50, then 75, upward to 100.

4 DOWN IN THE STRIKE ZONE

Objective: To keep the ball low in the strike zone.
Location: Anywhere on the field.
Technique: To practice throwing the ball on the low inside and low outside corners of the plate.

Procedure: Have athletes do the following—

- Pitchers pair off, stand about 60 feet apart, and take turns pitching and catching. Each hurler throws half an inning or three outs.
- The object is to throw knee-high pitches on the inside and outside corner of home plate. Use a rubber base for home plate.

Here are the game rules:

- A strike is any pitch that hits the low inside corner or low outside corner of home plate.
- A ball is any pitch that misses the target area.

- The pitcher throws to a hypothetical batter. Whenever he walks a batter, a run is charged against him. The catching partner calls balls and strikes.
- The game lasts three innings (optional). The athlete giving up the least number of runs wins the contest.

Comments: Tell pitchers to watch the target and follow through completely. Have pitchers throw at one-half to three-quarter speed.

An effective pitcher learns early to fire off the mound, field quickly, and make accurate throws to the basemen. The next two activities, Base Toss and Opposite Direction, offer practice in having pitchers fire off the mound.

5 BASE TOSS

Objective: To practice coming off the mound.
Location: Baseball diamond.
Technique: To practice staying alert, following through completely, and firing off the mound.

Procedure: Have athletes do the following—

- Four pitchers go to the diamond. Player 1 scatters three baseballs approximately 30 to 40 feet apart between the mound and home plate. Player 2 stands at first base, Player 3 goes to third base, and Player 4 stays near home plate.
- Action begins when Player 1, pitcher, winds up (without a ball) and simulates throwing a pitch to home plate. After the delivery he races toward the ball, fields it, and throws to first base. He returns to the mound, repeats the same procedure, and throws a ball to Player 3 and Player 4. The basemen return balls behind the pitcher's mound. Athletes rotate in order. Player 1 becomes Player 2, Player 2 becomes Player 3, and so forth. Have each athlete field and throw 9 to 12 balls.

Comments: Have pitchers sprint off the mound, field quickly, and concentrate on making accurate throws. Remind basemen to give a clear target. Caution pitchers to space balls far enough apart to prevent stepping on them.

6 OPPOSITE DIRECTION

Objective: To practice coming off the mound.
Location: Baseball diamond.
Technique: See Activity 5, Base Toss.
Procedure: Have athletes do the following—

- Four pitchers go to the diamond. Player 1 sets three base-balls along the first base line, about 20 feet apart, and three baseballs along the third base line, about 20 feet apart. Player 2 goes to first base, Player 3 stands behind the pitcher's mound about 10 feet in front of the second base bag. Player 4 goes to third base.
- Action begins when Player 1, pitcher, winds up (without a ball) and simulates throwing a pitch to home plate. After the delivery, he runs toward the first base line, fields each ball in turn, and throws to third base. The baseman tosses the balls to Player 3. Player 1 returns to the mound, simulates a pitch to home plate, runs toward the third base line, fields each ball in turn, and throws to first base. The baseman tosses the balls to Player 3. Athletes rotate in order. Player 1 becomes Player 2, Player 2 becomes Player 3, and so on. Have each athlete field and throw 12 balls.

Comments: See Drill 5, Base Toss.

Pitchers should try different methods for sharpening their control. Here are some popular techniques:

- The pitcher ties string (cord line) between two wooden poles in order to set up a target over home plate. He adjusts the string to cover the strike zone. A catcher wearing protective equipment goes to home plate. The pitcher throws balls to different spots within the target area.
- The hurler tapes or draws a strike zone against a wall. He throws a tennis ball or soft rubber ball at the target. NOTE: Some coaches do not want their pitchers to throw tennis balls. A smart pitcher who warms his arm properly, throws at half-speed, and doesn't try to break off curve balls should not strain his arm.
- The catcher moves his mitt around home plate, giving the pitcher different targets. The hurler pitches to one spot until he

can throw strikes consistently. The catcher then moves his target to a new area.

- A batter stands at home plate. He models different styles of hitting, e.g., open stance, closed stance, crouching at the plate, and so on. The pitcher and catcher combine strategy and work on the hitter's weakness. For example, if the catcher sees the hitter using a closed stance, he holds his glove on the low inside corner of home plate. NOTE: The batter does not swing at the pitch.

The next three activities show catchers how to block wild pitches, field bunted balls, and throw accurately to second base.

7 STOP THE BALL

Objective: To teach catchers the correct way to block poorly thrown baseballs.
Location: Baseball diamond, baseline areas, behind the backstop, or next to the boundary fences.
Technique: Stress is on blocking wild pitches thrown to the left, right, and in front of home plate. The following fundamentals help catchers block wild throws:

    A.   Balls thrown to the left of home plate.
        1. Move quickly to the left.
        2. Keep body in front of the ball.
        3. Drop to the right knee.
        4. Point the left knee toward third base.
        5. Keep the left shin guard pointing away from the pitched ball. This prevents the ball from bouncing off the shin guard.
        6. Place the mitt directly in front of the ball, tilting it slightly downward.
    B.   Balls thrown to the right of home plate.
        1. Move quickly to the right.
        2. Keep body in front of the ball.
        3. Drop to the left knee.
        4. Point the right knee toward first base.
        5. Keep the right shin guard pointing away from the pitched ball.

      6. Place the mitt directly in front of the ball, tilting it slightly downward.

C.   Balls bounding in front of the catcher.
1. Drop to both knees.
2. Keep body in front of the ball.
3. Place the mitt directly in front of the ball, tilting it slightly downward.

Procedure: Have athletes do the following—

- Catchers, wearing full protective equipment, pair off and stay 40 feet apart. They rotate between catching and pitching.
- Play begins as one of the catchers assumes the pitching role. He throws easy-to-handle pitches to the left, right, and in front of home plate. The tempo gradually increases, making throws harder to field. The catcher constantly shifts from right to left and left to right. After ten minutes, players change places and resume play. The catcher receives one point for each properly fielded ball. The catcher earning the most points becomes "Glove for a Day."

Comments: Catchers should practice fielding balls thrown at full speed. Throwing too easily encourages laziness.

    Start the drill with half-speed pitches over home plate. Gradually increase ball speed and move the pitches to the inside and outside corners of home plate. Catchers learn to move quickly in all directions. Then come way inside and outside of home plate with high and low pitches; include, also, bouncing balls in front of the catcher.

8 FIELDING THE BUNT

Objective: To teach catchers how to field bunted balls.
Location: Baseball diamond.
Technique: Fielding a bunted ball down the baseline is one of the toughest plays a catcher makes. A catcher must have quick reflexes and be a fast thinker. In this drill catchers emphasize fielding bunts down the third and first baselines in front of home plate. The following instructions help catchers achieve success:

A.   Bunted balls down the third baseline.
1. Fire out of the catcher's box.

2. Field the ball by scooping it up with bare hand and mitt.
3. Throw the ball only when the baseman is in position to make the catch.
4. Throw well inside the diamond to the baseman.

B. Bunted balls down the first baseline.
    The fundamentals are essentially the same as those for balls bunted down the third baseline.
C. Bunted balls in front of home plate.
    1. Charge the ball.
    2. Wave off the pitcher.
    3. Scoop up the ball with bare hand and mitt.
    4. Look at first base and throw.

Procedure: Have athletes do the following—

• Catchers, a first baseman, pitchers, a batter, and several runners participate. Place three baseballs 10 feet in front of home plate and three baseballs 20 feet along the third and first baselines. A batter steps into the batter's box. He squares around as if to bunt when the pitcher releases the ball. He makes no attempt to bunt the pitched ball. Runners line up to the right of the catcher's box.

Play starts when the pitcher delivers the ball to the catcher. He catches and tosses it over his shoulder to the backstop. The runner breaks for first base. The batter calls out "first," "third," or "home." Whatever the call, the catcher must field the ball in that area. Each catcher fields all 9 baseballs before changing off.

Comments: The catcher always locates the ball before throwing his face mask. Then he tosses it in the opposite direction. This prevents him from stepping on the mask and injuring an ankle. The catcher should know a runner's speed to determine the amount of time needed to make the play. He must concentrate on fielding the ball, not watching the runner.

9 STOP 'EM AT SECOND

Objective: To teach catchers how to throw accurately to second base.
Location: Baseball diamond.

Technique: Baserunners frequently steal on the pitcher who fails to keep them close to the bag. Clever baserunners get a good jump and break for second base the moment the pitcher motions toward home plate. This leaves little time for the catcher to throw out the advancing runner. The following techniques aid the catcher in throwing out the advancing runners:

1. After receiving the ball from the pitcher get rid of it quickly.
2. Shift body weight from the back to the front foot. Point the front foot in the direction of the throw.
3. Outstanding catchers can shift feet easily and smoothly. The pitch will determine if the catcher needs to shift. If shifting is necessary, it should be done quickly, smoothly, and with ease.
4. Come hard "out of the chute," that is, explode out of the catcher's box.
5. Grip the ball across the seams. This prevents the ball from sailing or tailing away from second.
6. Cock the throwing arm up over the ear. Throw with a complete follow-through of the arm. A good throw goes to the pitcher's glove side, shoulder-high.

Procedure: Have athletes do the following—

- Catchers, pitchers, shortstops, and second basemen participate. Runners line up near first base and take turns stealing second. Runners take a two-and-a-half-step lead and break for second the moment the pitcher motions toward home plate.
- The shortstop and second baseman alternate taking the throw from the catcher. When the shortstop receives the throw the second baseman backs up the play and vice-versa.
- Pitchers rotate throwing two or three pitches from a stretch motion. Play begins when the pitcher stretches, checks the runner, turns and throws the ball to the catcher. The runner breaks for second base. After receiving the ball the catcher throws hard to second base. Runners attempt to break up the play by upsetting the fielder or sliding around the tag. NOTE: The fielder should keep the fingers of his glove pointing toward the ground with the pocket facing away from the runner. This allows the ball and glove to give with a powerful slide and helps prevent hand and wrist injuries.
- If a runner is included, game conditions are simulated when the batter swings and misses. A swinging batter tests the

catcher's reflexes. He should rotate "batting" from each side of home plate.

Comments: Catchers should wear full protective gear, i.e., face mask, shin guards, chest protector, and supporting cup. If the pitcher wants to hold the runner close to the base, a first baseman enters the drill.

Here are four more activities that allow pitchers, catchers, and infielders to work together.

10 SCURRYING PITCHER

Objective: To practice the pitching motion.
Location: Baseball diamond.
Technique: The catcher acts as coach, watches the pitcher's delivery, and makes adjustments accordingly.

Procedure: Have athletes do the following—

- Pitchers and catchers pair off and stand about 60 feet away from each other.
- The pitcher concentrates on throwing strikes to the catcher. After each delivery, the catcher flips the ball to the right, to the left, or directly in front of the pitcher. The pitcher fields and again throws the ball to the catcher. The catcher watches the pitcher carefully and makes pitching corrections as needed.

11 FULL DELIVERY

Objective: To teach pitchers how to properly complete their delivery.
Location: Baseball diamond or warmup area.
Technique: Many pitchers fail to follow through completely, therefore remaining off balance after delivery. They are called "arm throwers" because they fail to bend their backs and push hard off the mound. A proper delivery requires the pitcher to finish by squarely facing the batter keeping his back parallel to the pitching mound. Body weight should be evenly distributed over both feet.

Procedure: Have athletes do the following—

- The coach, pitchers, and catchers participate. Draw a straight line in the dirt toward home plate (six feet long) from the center edge of the pitching rubber.
- Pitchers take turns, two throws each, winding up and throwing to the catcher. Pitchers stress bringing the lead foot quickly across the line slightly ahead of the delivery. The pitcher is in excellent fielding position to stop baseballs hit up through the middle of the diamond.
- When the pitcher releases the ball the coach throws bouncing ground balls back to the mound. The pitcher fields the balls and throws them back to the catcher. Each pitcher receives six to eight ground balls and alternates pitching from a set position and full windup.

Comments: Some pitchers need plenty of work on bringing the lead foot around quickly. A pitcher who follows through slowly, loses speed on the ball and has a difficult time responding to baseballs hit back through the box.

12 SIZING UP THE BATTER

Objective: To learn to spot batting weakness.
Location: Pitcher's mound or warmup area.
Technique: The drill's success hinges on pitcher/catcher savvy. Both pitcher and catcher study every batter who comes to the plate. Faults in his stance, grip, stride, or swing can give the pitcher enough ammunition to defeat him.

Procedure: Have athletes do the following—

- Catchers and pitchers participate. The coach or a designated player becomes a batter. He stands at home plate holding a bat and demonstrates different batting styles. As the batter changes positions, the catcher carefully watches for batting flaws.
- Pitchers concentrate hitting each target given by the catcher. The catcher moves his target according to the batter's weakness. Pitchers rotate every three or four pitches.

Comments: The batter's grip, stance, and swing are important features for the catcher/pitcher to study. A hitter using a tight grip on the bat will be unable to freely rotate his wrists and move the bat with a smooth, well-coordinated swing. An alert pitcher keeps his pitches to the inside corner of the plate. "Jamming" the hitter is smart pitching. Most batters drive inside pitches weakly onto the ground. A player uppercutting the ball pops up pitches thrown high or down the middle of the strike zone. A downward swing causes low-pitched balls to be grounded poorly into the infield.

The pitcher's strength lies in his ability to recognize individual batting weaknesses and to work with his catcher on pitching to these weak spots. A pitcher keeps hitters off balance by varying his pitches while throwing to these areas. Nearly all batters have an Achilles heel. The key is control: knowing a batter's weakness and being able to pitch to it are two different things.

13 OUT AT FIRST

Objective: To practice covering first base.
Location: Baseball diamond.
Technique: Whenever the batter hits a ball to the right side of the diamond, the pitcher should break to first base. The second baseman also breaks toward the first base side because he may have to field the ball if it is hit past the first baseman, who may be out of position to cover first. In this situation the second baseman fields the ball and tosses it to the pitcher. The pitcher breaks for the baseline, turns facing the bag, and runs parallel to the line. The baseman throws the ball chest-high so the pitcher sees the ball clearly. NOTE: Pitchers prefer a fairly hard toss. A soft throw is harder to handle.

Procedure: Have athletes do the following—

- Pitchers, catchers, first basemen, second basemen, and the coach take part. Each pitcher throws twice in succession.
- Play begins when a runner, simulating a batter, "swings" at the pitch and runs to first. The coach, standing behind the runner, hits a ground ball to the right side of first base. The pitcher breaks toward the baseline, turns toward first base when approximately three feet from the baseline, and runs parallel to the line until reaching the bag. He takes the throw from the baseman ahead of the runner. Pitchers receive six to eight chances.

Comments: The pitcher makes every attempt to avoid colliding with the runner. Running parallel with the baseline reduces the chance of collision.

INCLEMENT WEATHER ACTIVITIES

Here are three indoor activities for pitchers and catchers during inclement weather.

14 CATCHER'S GLOVE POINT GAME

Objective: To help pitchers develop control.
Location: Gymnasium.
Technique: Pitchers concentrate on hitting five major target areas in the strike zone.

Procedure: Have athletes do the following—

- Pitchers pair off taking turns throwing the ball to the catcher. The catcher assumes a crouching stance behind home plate (a movable rubber plate). The pitcher delivers the ball to the catcher's glove, which moves to different spots within the strike zone. Each pitcher throws an equal number of pitches from a windup and stretch position.

- The catcher gives five specific targets: high and low inside, outside corners, and directly over the center of home plate. After repeatedly hitting his target, the pitcher changes his style of pitches, e.g., fastball, curve, change-up, fastball, etc., and continues throwing.

Comments: Player interest increases when a point system is set up. Each pitcher receives one point per strike. The first player reaching 15 points wins. The catcher judges all pitches.

15 IN/OUT AND HIGH/LOW GAME

Objective: To help pitchers develop control.
Location: Gymnasium.
Technique: Pitchers concentrate on hitting high and low inside and outside corners of home plate.

Procedure: Have athletes do the following—

- Pitchers pair off. The catcher gives his target, and each pitcher takes turns throwing. The first pitcher hitting all four targets wins. A pitch down the middle receives no credit; it is considered the "no-no" zone.

Comments: Remind catchers to give a clear target while holding their mitts steady. A moving target creates confusion and may cause the pitcher to break his concentration.

16 COMING BACK IN A HURRY

Objective: To help develop quick reactions.
Location: Gymnasium.
Technique: Pitchers work together on their stance, windup, delivery, and follow-through.

Procedure: Have athletes do the following—

- A catcher, first baseman, coach, and pitchers participate. Pitchers rotate throwing and fielding. While one pitcher throws the remaining hurlers stay to the left and right of the pitcher. They retrieve any balls that go through the pitcher. Using three balls saves time chasing wild pitches.
- The pitcher winds up, throws the ball to the catcher, and immediately comes to a set fielding position. The coach, acting as a batter, hits a soft, rubber ball back at the pitcher (he doesn't hit the pitched ball). The pitcher fields the ball and throws it to first base. Pitchers alternate throwing from a windup and stretch position.

Comments: Pitchers must react quickly and stay alert. Each pitcher fields six batted balls. Players rotate either clockwise or counterclockwise. The coach hits hard line drives and ground balls, keeping each player on his toes.

chapter two

Infield Drills
and Games

An athlete doesn't become a good infielder overnight. He has to work hard—very hard—to perfect the skills necessary for successful team play.

Prior to infield drills, review the following points with your athletes:

- Keep body low by bending at the knees. Lower the buttocks and touch glove to the ground.
- Bring body weight forward, up over the balls of the feet. Keep feet comfortably spread with the left foot slightly forward of the right foot.
- Stay balanced. Be ready to move quickly to the left, to the right, or straight ahead.
- Fix eyes on the ball. Keep arms extended forward, palms turned inward, and fingers held together.
- After ball rolls into glove, trap it by bringing the throwing hand over ball. Draw glove to body, and bring arm back to throwing position.
- Release ball with a complete follow-through motion. Step toward the direction of the throw.

17 READY TO FIELD

Objective: To practice fielding ground balls properly.
Location: Any available area.

Technique: The infielder keeps his body leaning forward over the balls of his feet and low to the ground. His arms, flexed at the elbows, are well in front of the body while his feet are spread comfortably apart. This position allows him to back up, come forward, or go quickly to his right or left. An infielder can keep his body low by developing the habit of touching his glove to the ground. This practically forces him to remain low.

Procedure: The coach or player tosses fast low-bouncing or slow high-bouncing balls to the fielder. He fields and returns them to the thrower. Varying the ball speeds keeps the fielder alert.

Comments: Throwing a tennis ball against the garage door or inside the gym provides excellent practice. A player can combine fielding and throwing from different angles.

18 STAY LOW AND THROW

Objective: To practice fielding and throwing.
Location: Baseball diamond.
Technique: Athletes stay forward and extend their arms.

Procedure: Have athletes do the following—

- Go to the diamond. Split into two lines and form Groups A and B. Group A forms a line near third base; Group B gathers near first base. The coach and back-up man (manager or pitcher) come to home plate.

- Action begins when a Group A player takes a low fielding position to the left of third base. NOTE: Remind athlete to bend at the knees, keep body weight forward, and touch his glove to the ground. The coach rolls a slow bouncing ball to the fielder. When the coach yells, "Field," the player charges, scoops up the ball, and makes a throw to first base. A Group B player takes the throw. He returns the ball to the back-up man. After making the throw, Player A goes to line B; Player B goes to line A.

Comments: Let each athlete field and throw several times. Again, tell players to keep their weight forward and extend arms toward the ball. This helps keep the body in a low fielding position.

19 ATTACK

Objective: To practice fielding and throwing.
Location: Baseball diamond.
Technique: Athletes field and throw from a low fielding position.

Procedure: Have athletes do the following—

- Infielders line up near shortstop. The coach, back-up man (manager or pitcher), and runners come to home plate. The coach hits four balls, one at a time, to the left, to the right, or directly at the fielder. The athlete, assuming a low fielding position, must be ready for anything hit his way.
- Action begins when the coach hits a ball to the first fielder in line. A runner breaks for first base. He continues running the bases until he reaches home plate. The player fields and throws each ball to the back-up man.
- Award points in the following manner:

  1 point   Player fields cleanly and makes a good throw to the back-up man.

  2 points   The last throw beats the runner to home plate.

  If a player makes an error he loses all his points. The coach judges every play.

- Each athlete fields and throws four times before going to the end of the line. Optional: The game consists of two rounds or eight chances to field and throw. An athlete, playing two rounds, can score up to ten points.

Comments: Make sure runners wear protective equipment. Do not let runners slide into home plate. Advise the back-up man to stay behind home plate and not attempt to tag out the runner.

20 RUNNER ON THE GO

Objective: To practice fielding and throwing.
Location: Baseball diamond.
Technique: Athletes field and throw from a low fielding position.

Procedure: Have athletes do the following—

- Infielders, including pitcher and catcher, go to their positions. The coach and runners line up near home plate. SUGGESTION: Let extra players run the bases until they enter the drill.
- Action begins when the pitcher throws a ball to the catcher. When the ball reaches the catcher's mitt a runner breaks for first, and the coach fungos a ball to an infielder. The fielder must stop the runner from reaching base. If he succeeds, the runner returns to the line. If he fails, the runner goes to second base.
- Here are the rules for Runner on the Go:

  1. A runner is safe on an error or late throw.

  2. If a runner beats a throw to first he is awarded second base.

  3. The lead runner may advance only one base at a time. For example, a runner on second or third or runners at second and third advance to the next base if the runner going to first beats the throw or is safe on an error. If the runner makes an out players clear the bases and return to the line.

  4. A runner on third scores when the runner going to first reaches base safely.

  5. Runners advance one base on overthrows.

  6. The fielder tries to get the runner at first. He does not throw to any other base.

  7. After three outs runners clear the bases.

  8. When a runner scores, all infielders do five push-ups.

Comments: The success of the drill hinges on the coach's ability to place his hits. A ball that forces the fielder to run hard and throw quickly keeps the play close.

21 IN BETWEEN

Objective: To stress correct body position when fielding ground balls.
Location: Baseball diamond.
Technique: Players stay low to the ground with their hands outstretched in front of their bodies.

Figure 2-1
In Between

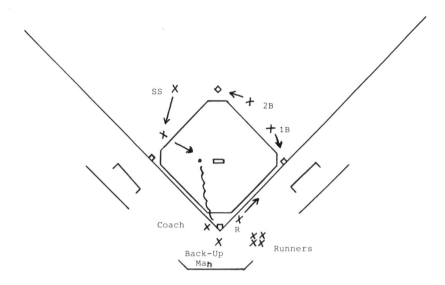

Procedure: Have athletes do the following—

- All infielders, excluding pitchers and catchers, take part.
- An extra player—pitcher—shags balls which go through the infield. Play begins when the coach hits a ground ball between two infielders. One fields, the other backs up the play. All throws go to the back-up man at home plate. **(See Figure 2-1.)**

Comments: After players have had several chances to field the ball, add runners and emphasize the importance of covering all bases.

22 PERFECTION

Objective: To practice making accurate throws to home plate.
Location: Baseball diamond.
Technique: The perfection in this drill comes when every infielder makes an accurate throw to home plate, knee-high and to the inside corner of home plate.

Procedure: This drill, used prior to regular infield practice, begins when the coach hits a ground ball to the third baseman. He fields and throws the ball to the catcher. If the play is successful, the next ball is hit to the shortstop, then to second, and so forth. The coach hits in succession to each member of the infield. If at any time a player misses or throws off-target to the catcher, the drill starts from the beginning and continues until all infielders perform flawlessly. All infielders receive a chance to field the ball regardless of when an error occurs. Allowances are made for bad hops or balls that are too hot to handle.

Comments: The catcher must be able to field all thrown balls with a minimum of effort. This type of throw during game competition allows the catcher to tag out a sliding runner. If the throw is low (belt-high to knee-level), the catcher is able to apply a direct tag.

23 ROCKET

Objective: To give infielders practice in charging, fielding, and throwing in one motion.
Location: Baseball diamond.
Technique: Each player quickly charges, fields, and throws the ball to first base. He doesn't have time to straighten up, plant his feet, and throw. Everything must be done in one continuous motion.

Procedure: Have athletes do the following—

- All infielders take their positions. Runners line up between home plate and first base, approximately 60 feet from first base.
- Play begins when the pitcher throws a ball to the catcher. The coach, standing at home plate, hits the ball to an infielder who makes the play at first.

Comments: Every player should receive several chances to field the ball. Knowing a hitter's speed and power can be of great advantage to the infielder. Runners are given a head start to encourage fielders to make quick plays. This is an excellent drill for back-up practice.

24 FULL SPEED AHEAD

Objective: To encourage players to charge the ball.
Location: Baseball diamond.

Technique: Inexperienced players develop the bad habit of waiting on the ball. They can break this habit by staying low, leaning forward, and quickly intercepting any ball hit to them.

Procedure: Have athletes do the following—

- All infielders, runners, and the coach participate.
- Play begins when the coach fungos three balls in succession to one of the infielders. The runner sprints to first base, rounds it, touches second, breaks for third, and slides into the bag. The fielder makes a throw to each base in turn, i.e., first, second, and third.

Comments: The coach must time the play so that each player can field the ball and make his throw slightly ahead of the runner.

Have the athletes compete in "Beat the Runner," a 12-point game. Each time an infielder's throw reaches a base ahead of the runner, award one point. An error—a bobbled ball or bad throw—wipes out the player's score.

Incorporate into outdoor station drills w/ adjustments.

25 ONE, TWO, THREE

Objective: To practice fielding and throwing.
Location: Baseball diamond.
Technique: Infielders work on proper fielding and throwing skills. They stay low, keep body weight forward, and make accurate throws to the glove side.

Procedure: Have athletes do the following—

- Infielders, excluding pitcher, go to their positions. Runners line up near first base. The coach brings a fungo bat to home plate.
- Action begins when a runner comes to first base. The coach hits three consecutive balls to the same fielder. (For example, he hits three balls to the first baseman before hitting to another baseman.) The runner goes from first base to second on the first hit, second to third on the second hit, and tags up from third on the last hit. NOTE: The runner, whether safe or out, stays on base. After touching home plate the runner goes to the end of the line. Play continues as another runner goes to first. *Runner either goes or tags*
- Chart 2–1 shows where the coach hits each ball and where players throw the ball.

CHART 2-1
ONE, TWO, THREE

Player	Ball	Where Coach Hits Ball	Where Players Throw Ball (Numbers Indicate Player Positions)
First baseman	1	Down first base line	To 6 covering second; 6 to 2
	2	Toward second base	To 5; 5 to 2 *NO*
	3	Fly to shallow right field *OR GROUNDER*	Runner tags up; 3 to 2
Second baseman	1	To the left of second base	To 6 covering second; 6 to 2
	2	Over second base bag	To 5; 5 to 2
	3	Fly to shallow center field	Runner tags up; 4 to 2
Shortstop	1	To the right of shortstop	To 4 covering second; 4 to 2
	2	Over second base bag	To 5; 5 to 2
	3	Fly to shallow center field	Runner tags up; 6 to 2
Third baseman	1	Down third base line	To 4 covering second; 4 to 2
	2	To the left of third base	To 6 covering third; 6 to 2
	3	Fly down the line in shallow left field	Runner tags up; 5 to 2

Comments: Make the activity last four rounds. Move at a slow pace until athletes become familiar with the routine. Allow runners to slide. Be sure runners and catcher wear protective equipment.

26 CHAMP OR CHUMP

Objective: To provide a fast-paced, interesting infield drill.
Location: Baseball diamond.

Technique: Infielders emphasize staying low, keeping their weight forward, and bending at the knees with arms outstretched in front of their bodies. The glove hand constantly touches the ground.

Procedures: Have athletes do the following—

- All infielders, excluding catchers, line up in a semicircle between second and third base. The coach stands between the pitcher's mound and the third baseline. A pick-up man (catcher) stands to the coach's right.
- The chump is a player who commits a throwing error or fumbles the ball. The champ is a player who performs flawlessly during the drill (or at least makes fewer errors than the other players). The objective is to become the champ by playing errorless ball. Clean fielding and throwing are necessary for success in this drill.

The rules are as follows:

1. Infielders must field and throw accurately to the pick-up man. A poorly thrown ball results in the infielder's becoming the chump.

2. The coach decides who will become champ or chump before the drill begins. The champ may be the player who won this title in a previous drill.

3. Play begins when the coach hits balls easily, then progressively livens up the drill by adding speed to ground balls. An infielder must play any type of ball hit into his area.

4. The infielder cannot pretend to field the ball or crowd another player. A violation of this rule results in the player becoming the chump.

5. If the ball is mishandled or thrown wild to the pick-up man, the player runs over to second base, touches the bag with his foot, sprints into left field and changes places with the chump.

6. Players move one position at a time from right or left (from the second toward third base) only when errors are made.

7. The chump acts as back-up for any balls hit through the legs or over the heads of the infielders. He can come back to the fielding zone when errors are committed. The chump takes his place at the end of the line (position nearest second base).

8. The champ can be dethroned only when he makes an error. Then he becomes the chump. The champ is subject to harder-

hit balls because his position is so close to the coach. Since he is champ, his right to the title is continually challenged.

9. Sharply hit balls or line drives deemed base hits are not recognized as errors. The coach serves as the judge.

Comments: The values obtained from this drill are threefold: (a) the coach controls the speed and type of ball he wishes to hit; (b) the infielders quickly realize that success comes only through sound utilization of fielding techniques; and (c) this drill motivates the players because it provides the incentive for becoming The Champ.

27 ONE STEP AHEAD

Objective: To stress getting rid of the ball quickly and accurate throwing.
Location: Baseball diamond.
Technique: Infielders throw the ball twice around the infield trying to beat the runner.

Procedure: Have athletes do the following—

- Infielders, excluding pitchers, take their positions.
- Runners line up at home plate. They go full speed around the bases one at a time. Play begins when the coach hits a ball to an infielder, for example, the third baseman. A runner heads for first and continues to round the bases. The baseman throws the ball to first base. From there it is relayed around the infield twice. The third baseman does not touch the ball the second time around. The player fielding the ball automatically drops out of the action when the ball goes around a second time. If the ball isn't dropped, bobbled, or wildly thrown, it will reach the catcher one step ahead of the average runner. Every infielder receives two chances to field the ball.

Comments: Pitchers make excellent baserunners. Any time a runner beats the ball around the infield, make all the infielders do five push-ups apiece. They'll work harder.

28 STOP 'EM

Objective: To practice throwing out runners.
Location: Baseball diamond.

Technique: Infielders practice throwing out advancing baserunners. They throw from different positions and at different speeds.

Procedure: Have athletes do the following—

- All infielders take their positions.
- Runners line up at home plate (outfielders). When the coach says, "Go," the lead runner breaks for first base and continues running until the play is completed. The coach, watching the runner, hits a ground ball, line drive, pop fly, high bouncer, and so forth, wherever he wishes. If the shortstop fields the ball and the coach yells, "Second," the shortstop throws the ball to second base. If the second baseman makes an error or the runner beats the throw, the guilty player does five push-ups.

Comments: Players will remain interested if the coach times his hitting with the runner's speed. Close plays are always exciting.

29 DEAD BALL

Objective: To stress quick thinking, fielding, and accurate throwing.
Location: Baseball diamond.
Technique: Players field and throw placed balls as directed.

Procedure: Have athletes do the following—

- The entire infield, including the pitcher and catcher, and the coach participate.
- Place two baseballs approximately six feet apart and ten feet ahead of each player. The coach, standing near home plate, yells "1 to 4 to 3, 6 to 4 to 3, 2 to 5 to 4," etc. These numbers indicate infield positions and tell players what to do, i.e., 5 to 4 to 3 means the third baseman charges, fields, and throws the ball to second base; the second baseman relays it to the first baseman who completes the double play. Each player fields both baseballs in his area. (**See Figure 2–2.**)

Comments: One way to develop quick thinking is to call out combined numbers such as 6–4–2, 1–5–4, 1–5–2, 6–2–3, etc. Also, make every erring player do five push-ups. This drill will work well with one ball. Caution players to avoid stepping on the balls.

Figure 2–2
Dead Ball

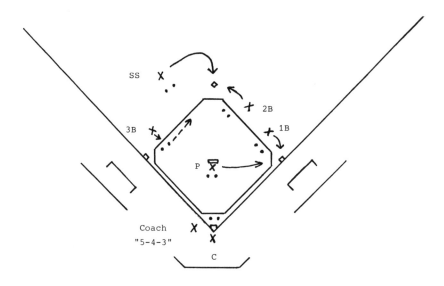

30 KEEP MOVING POINT GAME

Objective: To provide an interesting, fast-moving drill at the end of practice.
Location: Baseball diamond.
Technique: Players field ground balls, line drives, pop flies, and long fly balls.

Procedure: Have athletes do the following—

- Infielders form a single line between center field and second base. The coach and pick-up man (selected player) remain at home plate. On "Go," the first player breaks to his left. The coach hits a line drive, pop fly, ground ball, or long fly into right field. The player fields and throws the ball to the pick-up man.

- After each player takes several turns, vary hitting the ball straight away, to the right, sky high, and deep into the out-field.

- Score in the following manner: Give one point for ground balls, pop flies, and long fly balls. Award two points for a "circus catch." An error wipes out the score. The first player to earn ten points wins.

Comments: Emphasize clean fielding and accurate throwing to the pick-up man. Keep athletes moving briskly and challenge them by hitting balls which require a tough effort to field.

INCLEMENT WEATHER ACTIVITIES

Here are three indoor activities for infielders during inclement weather.

31 FIRST AND THIRD

Objective: To practice defending against the first and third situation, no outs.
Location: Gymnasium.
Technique: Infielders practice defensive and offensive skills.

Procedure: Have athletes do the following—

- Set up a baseball diamond. Use movable rubber bases.
- Select two teams of infielders, six players per team. Pitchers throw a tennis or rubber ball at half-speed. Catchers wear a face mask.
- Action starts when the defense, Team A, takes the field— catcher, pitcher, first baseman, second baseman, third baseman, shortstop. The offense, Team B, places runners at first and third; a batter comes to the plate. Situation: runners at first and third, no outs.
- The batter has two chances to advance the runners. If he swings and misses, takes a strike, or fouls the first pitch, he receives another delivery. If he fails to make contact, an out is recorded and players rotate; in other words, batter becomes first base runner, first base runner moves to third base, third base runner goes to the end of the line. The next batter in line steps up to the plate.
- The batter cannot walk or advance by being hit by the pitch. Runners may not lead off base but can steal when the opportunity arises. NOTE: The short distance between bases

restricts a baserunner's normal lead. However, through pre-arranged signals the batter and baserunner may combine offensive strategy, such as bunt and run, suicide, or safety squeeze, and so forth.

- The hitter has several options: he can take the first pitch, fake bunt, purposely swing and miss, bunt, or tap a ground ball onto the infield. He must use a choke grip with an easy swing. If he hits the ball over the infield, he's out, and runners cannot advance.
- Runners occupy first and third until the side is retired. Warn runners not to slide or interfere with play.
- After three outs the sides change. Team B takes the field; Team A comes to the plate. The catcher (designated player or coach) umpires the game. The team scoring the most runs wins.

Comments: The first and third play appears nearly every ball game. Athletes must be ready, offensively and defensively, to meet the situation. There are several methods of defense. The coach should choose those that fit his players' abilities and are easy to execute; too many variations only confuse athletes. This same principle applies to the offensive team. Athletes plan strategy according to the number of outs, player's ability, and inning. They learn which plays have the greatest chance of working.

32 DOUBLE UP

Objective: To practice fielding and throwing.
Location: Gymnasium.
Technique: Infielders practice their fielding, throwing, pivoting, and footwork skills.

Procedure: Have athletes do the following—

- Second basemen, shortstops, and runners take part.
- Set up a movable rubber plate (second base) approximately 70 feet from the gym wall. Runners (2 or 3) stand against the gym wall facing second base. The shortstop and second baseman take turns fielding and covering second base bag. The coach stands somewhere between second base and shortstop.

- Play begins when the coach throws a tennis ball against the wall. The shortstop fields the rebound and tosses the ball to the second baseman. The first runner in line breaks for second when the coach yells, "Go." Pitchers and outfielders make good baserunners. All runners return to the end of the line.
- After several repetitions the second baseman becomes the fielder. The coach continues to throw against the gym wall. The second baseman fields and throws the ball to the short-stop covering second base.
- Warn runners not to crash into the basemen or slide into second base. Include third basemen into the drill. Add another base and let them field rebounding balls off the wall.

Comments: The shortstop and second basemen practice footwork and develop split-second timing. The coach helps infielders with pivoting, fielding, and throwing techniques. Improving footwork should be part of every infielder's repertoire.

33 POP-THE-TARGET GAME

Objective: To practice fast fielding and throwing.
Location: Gymnasium.
Technique: Infielders practice fielding and throwing in one swooping motion.

Procedure: Have athletes do the following—

- All infielders take part.
- Tape a target area, three feet by one foot, on the gym wall. Keep the bottom line of the target at least three feet above the gym floor. The target represents a first baseman's glove.
- The coach (or designated player) stands to one side of the target. He judges all thrown balls.
- Infielders (Player 1) line up around second base (a movable rubber plate), and stay about 60 feet to the right of the target.
- Send one player (Player 2) approximately 100 feet ahead, directly facing the target. His job is to recover the rebounds. Send another player (Player 3) 60 feet ahead, and directly facing the infielders (Player 1).

- When the coach hollers, "Go," Player 3 rolls a tennis or rubber ball slowly toward Player 1. Player 1, running at full speed, cups his hands, scoops, and throws with an underhand motion at the target. Player 3 has two choices: he can roll the ball along the floor or he can throw a slow bouncer.
- After throwing the ball, Player 1 becomes Player 2; Player 2 becomes Player 3; and Player 3 goes to the end of the line.
- Award points as follows:

3 points	Player fields cleanly and makes a good throw inside the taped boundaries.
2 points	Player fields cleanly and hits the taped boundary.
1 point	Player fields cleanly but misses the target.
0 points	Player bobbles the ball.

- The first player earning 12 points wins.

Comments: There are occasions when an infielder doesn't have time to charge, pick up the ball, get set, and throw. He must make the play in one swooping motion. Remind players never to attempt this play if a wild throw would score the winning run.

This drill points up two important factors: off-balance throws are extremely difficult to make, and oftentimes costly. A player must stay in a low fielding position and never take his eyes off the ball.

chapter three

Outfield Drills
and Games

BEGIN WITH THE PROPER GRIP

Many outfielders take pride in throwing baserunners out with their strong, powerful arms. Unfortunately, not all outfielders possess rocket arms. In fact, some sacrifice accuracy for strength by trying to throw the ball too hard.

An outfielder should master gripping the ball properly and making throws with a complete follow-through motion before concentrating on strength activities.

Admittedly, the grip represents only one small part of the throwing action, but if done incorrectly, it can mean the difference between winning and losing the game. For example, an outfielder attempts to throw a runner out at home plate. The ball sails to the right forcing the catcher to leap for the ball. The catcher, forced out of position, fails to tag out the runner.

Here are three ways to find out if outfielders grip the ball properly: (1) Watch how catchers and infielders position their bodies before and after tagging runners. If an outfielder's throw pulls them off base, chances are the ball sailed to the left or right; (2) Ask infielders if the ball came in on a straight line or veered to one side; (3) Ask each outfielder, in turn, to show you how he grips the ball. NOTE: Keep in mind that an outfielder may use a different grip when hurrying to throw out a runner.

The proper cross seam grip requires a player to do the following:

- Place first and second fingers across the seams of the ball. Keep both fingers about one-half inch apart.
- Let the ball rest over the thumb. The third finger helps the thumb hold up the ball.
- Make sure the ball stays forward, away from the palm.
- When releasing the ball use the first two fingers to push the ball away from the hand.

The following two drills stress using a cross seam grip.

34 THINK CROSS SEAM

Objective: To concentrate on using a cross seam grip.
Location: Outfield area.
Technique: How to throw using a cross seam grip.

Procedure: Have athletes do the following—

- Pair off and throw to each other.
- Take turns throwing overhand at the shoulder area of partner. NOTE: Athletes should apply a cross seam grip without looking at the ball. A complete follow-through adds to the accuracy of each toss.
- Slowly move apart by stepping backwards, increasing the distance until partners are about 150 feet away from each other.
- Throw the ball 10 feet in front of partner. A proper cross seam grip allows the ball to follow a direct path in flight, that is, it will not curve, twist, or slide. After the ball hits the ground the single bounce carries it directly to the receiver.
- Move apart until partners are approximately 250 feet away from each other. Add a third player (outfielder, pitcher, etc.) to act as a cut-off man.

Comments: The outfielders' throws should be free from sideward rotation.

35 QUICK TARGET
(a competitive throwing game)

Objective: To concentrate on using a cross seam grip.
Location: Outfield area.
Technique: How to throw using a cross seam grip. NOTE: This drill requires players to make rush throws. Have athletes concentrate on making accurate throws by keeping their eyes on the target and thinking cross seam grip.

Procedure: Have athletes do the following—

- Form a single line. A designated player stands about 100 feet in front of the first person in line. He stands with a fence, net, or screen at his back. He faces the line and holds his glove shoulder high. **(See Figure 3–1.)**
- The designated player yells "Go" and tosses a ball to the left, right, or directly in front of the first player in line.

Figure 3–1
Quick Target

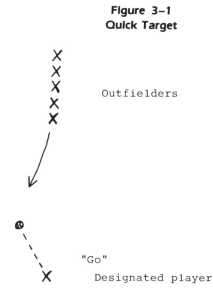

X
X
X   Outfielders
X
X

            "Go"
X   Designated player

XXXXXXXXXXXXXXXXXXXXXXXXX Fence, net or screen

- The player fields the ball, applies a cross seam grip, and throws it at the designated athlete's glove. The fielding athlete has two choices: throw the ball on the line with no bounce or one-hop the ball.
- After the player fields and throws the ball he switches places with the designated player. The designated player goes to the end of the line.
- Every player should field and throw four or five times before playing Quick Target.

Here's how to play Quick Target:

- Repeat the same procedure with one exception: If the throw goes awry—too wide, low, or high—the designated player makes no attempt to catch it. He lets it go to the fence or screen. The fielding player recovers the ball and becomes the designated player.
- The designated athlete acts as judge; he decides whether a throw is on-target or not. He also awards points as follows:

2 points	Bulls-eye. The designated player didn't have to move his glove.
1 point	The designated player has to move his glove less than one foot, but more than six inches to catch the ball.
0 points	The ball misses the target by more than one foot.

- Each player keeps track of his own score.
- The first player to earn 10 points wins the game. Honesty, of course, is the key to success.

Comments: Play the game as long as player interest holds out. However, a good time to quit and do something else is when athletes reach a peak or demonstrate a high-anxiety level.

FINISH WITH A COMPLETE FOLLOW-THROUGH

Once an outfielder masters the cross seam grip he should concentrate on coordinating his arm and body motion together in a smooth manner to keep the ball on target.

A conscientious athlete can develop a graceful follow-through if he practices these steps (right-handed thrower):

- When beginning the throwing motion, point front or pivot foot toward the target.
- Draw arm back. Keep elbow even with shoulder. Be careful not to let arm drop.
- Shift hips and shoulders to throwing side of body. Swing body weight over front foot.
- Lift and extend left foot toward target. Reach back with throwing arm.
- Shift body weight from pivot to left leg as ball leaves hand.
- Release the ball with a complete follow-through motion. The wrist should snap in a downward motion on the follow-through.

36 TOUCH THE TURF

Objective: To practice throwing the ball with a complete follow-through motion.

Location: Outfield area.

Technique: The player fields, grips (cross seam), and throws the ball with a complete follow-through of the body. Every outfielder emphasizes bringing his throwing arm overhand. After releasing the ball head-high, he follows through by contacting the ground with his fingertips, hence touching the turf.

Procedure: Have athletes do the following—

- Form a straight line. Select a player to act as catcher for balls thrown by outfielders. The designated catcher should stand about 150 feet away and face outfielders.
- The coach (or designated athlete) stands to the left of the catcher. He starts the drill by yelling, "Go" and hits a fungo to the left or right of the first player in line.
- The player fields and throws the ball to the catcher. After he releases the ball he must follow through by touching the ground and picking up dirt or grass. This move forces the player to follow through completely. He then tosses the dirt or grass into the air to show that he actually touched the turf.

- The fielding player returns to the end of the line.
- Each outfielder should field and throw four or five times.

Comments: After an athlete touches the ground he should immediately look at the catcher and study his throw. This allows the fielder to retain body balance.

37 RUMPLE THE TOWEL
(a competitive throwing game)

Objective: To practice making single-bounce throws.
Location: Outfield area.

Figure 3–2
Rumple the Towel

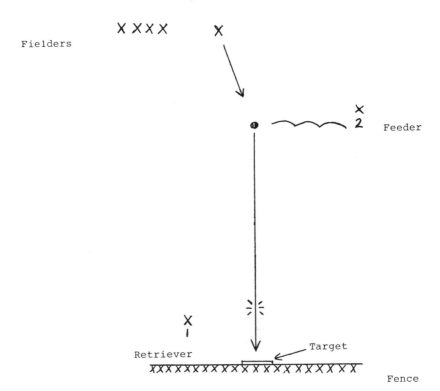

Technique: The player fields, grips (cross seam), and throws the ball with a complete follow-through motion.

Procedure: Have athletes do the following—

- Go to an open area in the outfield. Stand about 150 to 200 feet away from a sideline fence.

- The coach or designated player ties a cloth towel (two feet by one foot in size) on the fence approximately three feet above the ground. The towel gives the outfielders a throwing target. Player 1, the retriever, collects the balls thrown into the fence. He also judges each thrown ball. Player 2, the feeder, tosses balls to the fielder. He stands about 50 feet in front of the fielders. **(See Figure 3–2.)**

- Action begins when the feeder calls "Go." He tosses a ball in front of the fielder. NOTE: The feeder may throw a fly ball or a ground ball. The player fields and makes a single-bounce throw to the target. If the ball strikes the target, the fielder receives two points. Each athlete makes 3 throws before rotating in the following manner: Fielder becomes retriever, retriever becomes feeder, and feeder goes to the end of the fielding line. The outfielder who earns the most points wins.

Comments: Remind outfielders to use a cross seam grip and throw overhand with a complete follow-through.

38 ONE-HOPPER

Objective: To practice fielding and throwing.
Location: Outfield area.
Technique: Each player breaks, runs at full speed, fields and throws the ball. Players stress making single-bounce throws.

Procedure: Have athletes do the following—

- Separate into four stations. **(See Figure 3–3.)** The coach and back-up man (extra outfielder) stay near the left field foul line.

- Play begins when the coach says, "Break." The first fielder at station 1 runs at full speed toward center field. The coach hits a long fly, line drive, or fast, bouncing ground ball. Player 1 fields and throws a single-bouncer or one-hopper to Player 2. Player 2 relays a single-bouncer to Player 3, and so on.

Figure 3–3
One-Hopper

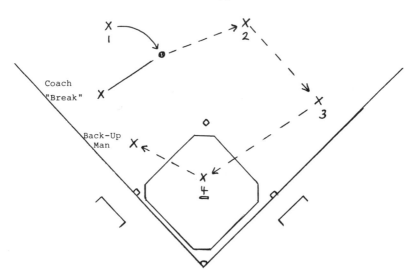

- Athletes move clockwise taking turns fielding and throwing. Erring players do 10 push-ups or some other mild "penalty."

Comments: Some coaches prefer not to use push-ups for punishment. Before the drill begins, have athletes decide what penalty erring players should pay.

39 TESTING THE THROWING ARM

Objective: To find strong throwing arms.
Location: Infield/outfield area.
Technique: Each outfielder makes hard, overhand throws with a complete follow-through.

Procedure: Have athletes do the following—

- Infielders take their positions. Outfielders line up in right field. Runners (extra players) gather near first base and the coach comes to home plate. **(See Figure 3–4.)**
- Action begins when a runner goes to first base. The coach fungos a base hit to right field. The first outfielder in line fields and

Figure 3–4
Testing the Throwing Arm

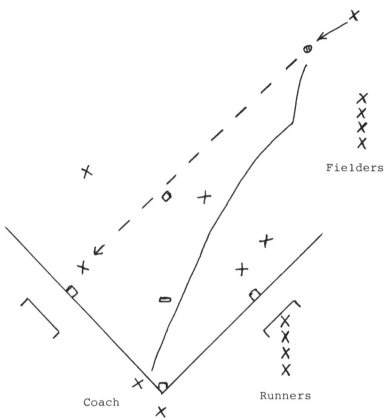

throws to third base. NOTE: Tell the runner to sprint full-speed to third. After the play the runner goes to the end of the line.

• Give outfielders several chances to field and throw.

Comments: The man-on-first, base-hit-to-right situation occurs frequently. It takes a strong arm to cut the runner down at third. This drill helps the coach find a strong-throwing right fielder. The second baseman stays near the bag. Since the outfielder throws to third, the second baseman doesn't have to enter short right field to become a relay man. If the ball gets by the outfielder the baseman runs into right field and takes the relay. The shortstop acts as cut-off man for the outfielder. The third baseman tells the shortstop how to line up. The pitcher backs up third base.

40 STILL-BALL THROW

Objective: To develop quick thinking in fielding and throwing.
Location: Baseball diamond.
Technique: On the coach's command the outfielder charges, fields, and throws a placed ball to the back-up man.

Procedure: Have athletes do the following—

- Go to their respective positions in the outfield.
- Place a ball fairly deep between left-center and center-right. The coach and back-up man (extra outfielder) stay near the pitcher's mound.
- The coach begins play by calling out 787, 788, 898, or 899. The first two numbers indicate field position. The remaining number represents the fielding player. For example, if the coach calls out "787," the left-fielder charges, picks up, and throws the ball (resting between left and center field) to the back-up man. The center fielder backs up the left fielder.
- After everyone fields the ball at least once, they rotate moving clockwise, i.e., the right fielder becomes the back-up man, the back-up man goes to left field, and so forth.

Comments: The coach is in an excellent position to make fielding and throwing corrections.

41 FLIP AND SHOOT

Objective: To practice making overhand throws to home plate.
Location: Baseball diamond.
Technique: Each outfielder makes hard, overhand throws with a complete follow-through.

Procedure: Have athletes do the following—

- Outfielders and infielders go to their positions. Outfielders, playing medium deep, bring a ball with them. Runners (extra players) gather near second base. NOTE: Use only two or three runners at a time. The coach stands behind the pitcher's mound.

- Action begins when the coach yells, "Go," and the runner takes off for third. The left fielder tosses a ball several feet to his left or to his right, charges the ball, fields, and throws the ball to home plate. The runner tries to score on the play.
- Play continues as the center fielder and right fielder follow the same procedure. Let each outfielder make three or four throws. The cut-off men return balls to the outfielders.

Comments: Have the third baseman cut off throws from left field, and the first baseman cut off throws from center and right. Be sure catcher and runners wear protective equipment. Allow slow runners to get a good jump from second base.

42 RELAY DRILL

Objective: To teach outfielders teamwork in fielding.
Location: Baseball diamond.
Technique: Outfielders practice fielding, relaying, and throwing the ball to the back-up man.

Procedure: Have athletes do the following—

- Outfielders go to their positions. The coach and back-up man (pitcher) remain at home plate.
- The coach starts play by hitting long, hard drives between left-center and right-center. The player closest to the ball fields it while the player farthest away turns and runs toward the infield. He becomes the relay man for the fielder.

Comments: Two outfielders trying to pick up one ball at the same time wastes valuable energy. If the fielder closest to the ball yells out, "I'll take it," and waves off the other outfielder, considerable time and energy will be saved.

43 CLEAN FIELDING GAME

Objective: To practice fielding and throwing.
Location: Outfield area.

Procedure: Have athletes do the following—

- Outfielders go to the field and line up. The coach and back-up man (manager or pitcher) stand about 150 feet away.
- Action begins when a player takes his fielding stance. Each athlete must do these three things:
  1. Crouch low, keeping body weight forward.
  2. Keep arms extended out in front of body.
  3. Remain still until the coach hits the ball.
- The coach fungos a ball to the first fielder in line. After the ball leaves the bat, the coach yells, "Go," and the player fields and throws to the back-up man. Award points as follows:

1 point	Athlete makes a routine play, for example, catches a pop fly or fields a ground ball.
2 points	Athlete makes a shoestring catch or a leaping overhead catch.

- The first player earning 15 or more points wins. An athlete loses his points if he moves before the coach hollers, "Go," makes a fielding error, or makes a poor throw to the back-up man. After the play the fielder goes to the end of the line.

Comments: Give each player several turns. Repeat the activity often.

44 WHERE IS IT?

Objective: Outfielders stress catching fly balls while staying high on their toes.

Location: Outfield area.

Technique: A flat-footed runner (heel-to-toe stepper) usually has trouble judging a fly ball. His jerky steps cause his head to bounce up and down. He's never sure what path the ball is taking. An outfielder should catch fly balls with his body weight slightly forward over the balls of his feet. This keeps his head fairly still when running.

Procedure: Have athletes do the following—

- Outfielders line up near the left field foul line. The coach and back-up man (pitcher) stand approximately 70 feet to the right of the players.

- The coach yells "Go" and the first player in line runs straight ahead approximately 50 feet. He concentrates on keeping his weight distributed over both feet. The coach hits a towering fly ball into the air. The fielder locates, catches, and throws it to the back-up man. He returns to the end of the line.

Comments: Have athletes concentrate on these fundamentals— After locating the ball, take a comfortable position under it. Make the catch with hands outstretched over and forward of the head. After catching the ball, quickly get rid of it.

45 COMING AT YOU

Objective: To teach correct glove position in fielding.
Location: Outfield area.
Technique: A player points the glove fingers down and turns the palm up when catching balls hit below the waist. He points the glove fingers up and turns the palm down when catching balls hit above the waist.

Procedure: Have athletes do the following—

- Outfielders form a single line in center field. The coach and back-up man (pitcher) stand approximately 100 feet away facing them.
- When the coach calls out, "Charge," the first player in line runs at full speed toward the coach. The coach lashes a hard line drive back at the player. The player fields and fires the ball (shoulder-high) at the back-up man. He returns to the end of the line.

Comments: Athletes must stay alert and move quickly. They learn the value of playing "heads-up" ball.

46 MOVE IT OUT

Objective: To give outfielders experience in running long distances for fly balls.
Location: Outfield area.
Technique: The outfielder learns only through experience where a long fly ball will land. He must decide, turn, and quickly run to the

spot where he thinks the ball will land. At the last moment he looks up, locates, and catches the ball.

Procedure: Have athletes do the following—

- Line up in left field facing the infield. The coach and back-up man (pitcher) stay near the left field foul line.
- On the signal, "Go," the first player in line runs at full speed toward right field. The coach hits a long fly ball into right field. The player locates and catches the ball. He throws a single-bouncer into the back-up man and returns to the end of the line.

Comments: This drill tests the stamina, patience, and enthusiasm of the athletes. A hard-working, hustling player will know he's been through a test.

47 LONG FLY BALL

Objective: To practice catching balls hit over the fielder's head.
Location: Outfield area.
Technique: See Drill 46, Move It Out.

Procedure: Have athletes do the following—

- Outfielders go to the field. The back-up man (pitcher or manager) stays near the coach. A relay man stands between the fielder and back-up man.
- Action begins when the coach fungos a long fly ball over the fielder's head. The fielder turns and runs to where he thinks the ball will land. He stops, turns around, and faces the ball. After catching the ball the player makes an overhand throw to the relay man. Award points as follows:

0 points	Misjudges ball, for example, stops too soon or runs too far. Ball either drops in front of player or lands behind him.
1 point	A player takes four steps or less after turning around to catch the ball.
2 points	A player takes two steps or less after turning around to catch the ball.
4 points	A player fields the ball in the spot where he turns around to make the catch.

Rule   A player cannot watch the ball while running after it. If he does, he loses all of his points.

Comments: Athletes judge one another. Each player keeps track of his own score. Give each athlete several turns. Players rotate after every play, for example, fielder becomes relay man and relay man goes to the end of the line. The athlete with the most points wins.

48 THREE BALL

Objective: To practice fielding and throwing.
Location: Outfield area.
Technique: Outfielders practice fielding and making accurate overhand throws to the glove side of the relay man.

Procedure: Have athletes do the following—

- Outfielders go to the field. A player, the relay man, positions himself between the outfielders and coach. A back-up man (manager or pitcher) stands to the right of the coach. **(See Figure 3–5.)**
- Action begins when the coach fungos three balls, one at a time, to the first outfielder in line. Chart 3–1 shows the hitting, fielding, and throwing patterns.
- On the third hit the relay man drops into cut-off position by running toward the back-up man. The back-up man tells the relay man how to line up, for example, to the left or to the right. The fielders make a shoulder-high overhand throw to the glove side of the relay man.

CHART 3-1

Ball	Where Coach Hits Ball	Where Fielder Throws Ball
1	Ground ball to fielder's right	To the back-up man
2	Ground ball to fielder's left	To the back-up man
3	High fly to fielder	To the relay man

Figure 3–5
Three Ball

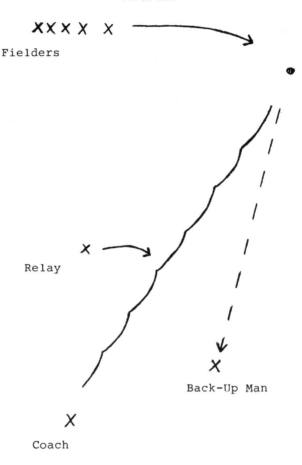

X X X X   X
Fielders

Relay

Back-Up Man

X
Coach

- After the play the fielder becomes the relay man, and relay man goes to the end of the fielder's line.

Comments: Have athletes field and throw several times. Stress the importance of making good throws to the relay man.

49 THREE IN LINE

Objective: To practice fielding and throwing.
Location: Baseball diamond.

Technique: Outfielders practice fielding and making accurate overhand throws to the glove side of basemen. Infielders practice cutting off throws from the outfield and tagging runners.

Procedure: Have athletes do the following—

- Infielders go to their positions. Outfielders line up in left field and the coach stands near home plate.
- The shortstop sets three balls in a line about 20 feet apart and approximately 100 feet behind second base. Runners (extra players) line up at home plate. **(See Figure 3–6.)**
- Action begins when a runner comes to home plate. When the coach yells, "Go," the runner takes off and the first outfielder in line sprints toward Ball 1. He picks it up and makes a play on the runner. If the fielder throws out the runner, the runner returns to the end of the line. If the runner is safe, he stays on base. The fielder returns to his starting position and repeats the same procedure for Ball 2 and Ball 3.

Figure 3–6
Three In Line

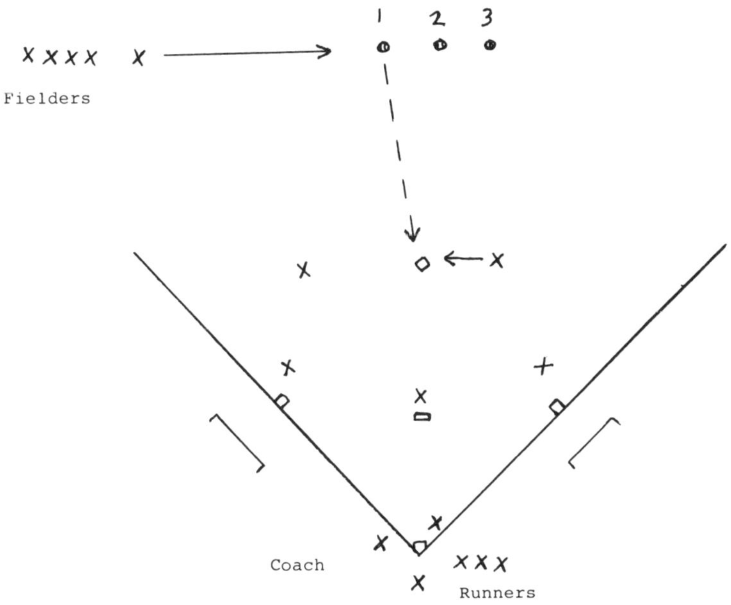

- The athlete fields all three balls consecutively before going to the line. The pitcher collects returning balls, throws them to the shortstop, and the shortstop replaces each ball for the next fielder.

Comments: Infielders receive excellent base coverage practice. The coach can stop play and make corrections at any time. Have the third baseman act as cut-off man for Ball 1; the first baseman cuts off Ball 2 and Ball 3. Let runners lead off from base. Make sure the catcher and runners wear protective equipment. Remind outfielders to think ahead and make overhand throws to the correct base.

50 SUPREME SACRIFICE GAME

Objective: To encourage outfielders to become more aggressive.
Location: Outfield area.
Technique: This drill emphasizes blocking bounding balls, charging slow-hit balls, and properly trapping the low line drive. Supreme Sacrifice requires an outfielder to leave his feet and dive for the ball.

Procedure: Have athletes do the following—

- Outfielders form a line in right field approximately 100 feet away from and facing the coach. The coach and back-up man (pitcher) stay to the inside of the right field foul line. (**See Figure 3–7.**)

- All players compete and collect points for successful fielding. Award points as follows:

A routine ground or fly ball	1/2 point
A hard line drive	1 point
A play requiring fielder to trap ball	1 point
Supreme Sacrifice—A ball requiring fielder to make a diving "shoestring" catch.	2 points

- The first player to earn 10 points wins. If an error occurs at any time during this drill, the erring player loses all points earned up to that point and must start over again. The coach judges all plays.

Comments: This is a highly successful drill because:

Figure 3–7
Supreme Sacrifice Game

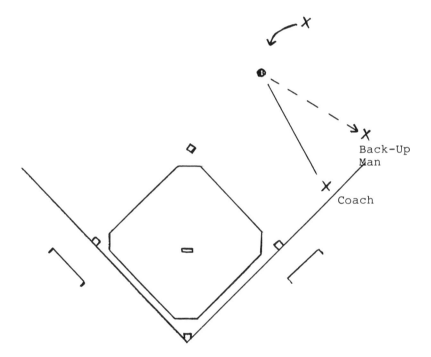

- Each outfielder concentrates on batted balls hit at various speeds in different directions.
- Outfielders attempt to catch baseballs that ordinarily drop to the ground for base hits.

INCLEMENT WEATHER ACTIVITIES

Here are three indoor activities for outfielders during inclement weather.

51 FACE THE MUSIC
(point game)

Objective: To practice fielding and throwing.
Location: Gymnasium.
Technique: Outfielders practice making accurate throws and fielding balls coming directly at them.

Procedure: Have athletes do the following—

- Outfielders divide into two groups—six to eight per group. Each group takes a tennis ball or soft rubber ball and goes to a different area of the gymnasium.
- Groups break into two teams, A and B. Players line up about 30 feet from the gymnasium wall. Groups remain several feet apart.
- Action begins when Player A tosses the ball at eye level against the gymnasium wall; Player B fields the rebound.
- Player B receives points for accurate fielding based on the following point scheme:

Line drive	1 point	Player must catch the ball in flight.
Single-bounce	1 point	Player traps or fields the ball after it hits the floor in front of him.
Grounder	½ point	Player fields the ball after it strikes the ground two or more times.

- If the player makes an error any time during the game he loses all points and must start over again. If Player A makes a bad throw which causes the ball to deflect to one side or bounce high in the air, Player B receives a ½ point bonus. He also receives another turn. Player A loses ½ point from his total score.
- After Player A throws the ball, he must not interfere with Player B. If any player interferes with Player B, Player B receives 1 point plus another turn. The infracting player loses 1 point from his total score.
- After throwing the ball, Player A goes to the end of Line B; Player B moves to the end of Line A. The first athlete to earn 10 points wins.

Comments: Check the gym wall surface for anything which may cause the ball to deflect or bounce high in the air. Lay a strip of tape at eye level across the wall. This gives players a target and helps them make accurate throws.

52 QUICK SPIN

Objective: To practice fielding and throwing.
Location: Gymnasium.
Technique: Athletes practice making quick turns, finding the ball, and fielding to their right or left.

Procedure: Have athletes do the following—

- Follow the same procedure outlined in Drill 51, Face the Music. Make these additions:

    1. Player B turns his back to the wall. When Player A throws the ball against the wall, Player B quickly spins around, locates the ball, and fields the rebound.

    2. Player A throws the ball against the gymnasium floor approximately one to two feet in front of the wall. He adjusts his tosses according to the type of rebound desired, for example, if he wants a high, lofty fly ball, he throws the ball hard against the floor. If he wants a soft bouncer or fly ball, he throws the ball easily against the floor.

    3. Combine Face the Music (Drill 51) and Quick Spin. Players must stay alert and be ready to move in any direction.

53 ONE BOUNCE

Objective: To practice fielding and throwing.
Location: Gymnasium.
Technique: Outfielders concentrate on clean fielding and making overhand, shoulder-high throws to the glove side.

Procedure: Have athletes do the following—

- Outfielders form a single line facing the gymnasium wall. They should be at least 90 to 100 feet from the wall.

- Tape a target area on the gymnasium wall, approximately three feet long by two feet wide. The bottom line of the target should be two or three feet from the gymnasium floor.

- Player A (coach) stands in front of the target, his back turned to the wall. He judges all thrown balls. Another athlete, Player B, stands about 40 to 50 feet away from and directly in line with the target. He represents the cut-off man. (Optional: Use infielders for cut-off men.)

- Action starts when Player B throws a tennis ball or soft rubber ball—either a bouncer or a fly—to the first player in line, Player C. The player fields and throws the ball to the cut-off man.

- Player B lines up between Player A and Player C. Player A tells Player B which way to move when Player C throws the ball, for example, left or right.

- Player C concentrates on throwing the ball shoulder high and to the glove side of Player B. A good throw will bounce once before hitting the gym wall.

- Player B stops off-target throws when Player A yells, "Cut." If Player A says nothing, the ball is allowed to go through.

- Play "Target Eight." Scoring is as follows:

0 points	Players receive no points for wild or off-target throws.
1/2 point	Ball hits the taped margin which surrounds the target.
1 point	Ball lands inside the taped boundaries.
– 1 point	Player C loses a point if he fails to follow through with an overhand throw or throws the ball sidearm.

- Player C makes two throws, then becomes Player B; Player B goes to the end of the line. Player B recovers the ball and gives it to Player C. The first player to earn eight points wins.

Comments: A shoulder-high, glove-side throw to the cut-off man saves time and makes ball handling easier. An overhand toss with a complete follow-through adds power to the throw.

chapter four

Hitting
and Bunting
Drills and Games

Possibly the single toughest skill in baseball to teach is hitting. A batter, like a computer, is most effective when all of his circuits are working. The stance, stride, and swing make up a large part of this circuitry.

An alert coach watches his hitters carefully. He realizes that finding and correcting batting flaws can be extremely difficult. One problem a coach faces is overcoaching, i.e., confusing the athlete by having him work on too many things at once. Perhaps the best remedy is to have the athlete concentrate on one thing at a time until he gains confidence in his hitting ability.

54 TWO-MAN SLAM

Objective: To practice hitting the ball.
Location: Sideline fence area.
Technique: Athletes hit a lobbed pitch into the sideline fence. They concentrate on keeping their eyes on the ball and following through with a smooth, level swing.

Procedure: Have athletes do the following—

- Two athletes, Player 1 and Player 2, take turns hitting the ball into the fence. Player 1, the hitter, stands about 20 feet from

CHART 4–1

Station	Time (min.)	Location	Player Responsibility
1	5	Home plate	Hits live pitches
2	5	Behind batting cage	On deck batter: swing a bat, stretch out
3	5	Right sideline fence	Hits off a batting tee
4	5	Right sideline fence	Tosser for Two-Man Slam (Drill 54)
5	5	Right sideline fence	Hitter for Two-Man Slam (Drill 54)
6	5	Left field foul line	Back-up man for outfield fungoer (Station 7)
7	5	Left field foul line	Fungo balls to outfielders
8	5	Left side of batting cage	Back-up man for infield fungoer (Station 9)
9	5	Left side of batting cage	Fungo balls to infielders

the sideline fence. Player 2, the tosser, stays to one side and faces Player 1.

- Play begins as Player 2 signals, "Ready," and lobs the ball to Player 1. The batter hits the ball into the fence. Each player hits several balls apiece.

Comments: Have the tosser stand to the right of right-handed hitters and to the left of left-handed hitters. Use worn, scuffed balls.

55 FIVE-MINUTE HIT

Objective: To combine hitting and fielding.
Location: Baseball diamond.

Technique: Players work on their stance, stride, and swing. Fielders concentrate on staying low, fielding cleanly, and throwing accurately.

Procedure: Have athletes do the following—

- Divide the team into two groups, A and B, with nine players (optional) per group. Keep each team balanced, for example, pitcher, catcher, four infielders, and three outfielders.

- Group A, the offense, comes to bat with each athlete spending five minutes at a different station. Chart 4–1 shows the station, time, location, and player responsibility.

- Group B athletes, the defense, play their regular positions. They work on fielding techniques. Infielders practice fielding, throwing, setting up relays, and cutting off throws from the outfield. Outfielders practice catching fly balls, fielding ground balls, backing up each other, and making overhand throws.

- The pitcher throws one-half to three-quarter speed. He alternates pitching from a stretch and wind-up position. The catcher, wearing full protective gear, moves his target around the strike zone. SUGGESTION: Let pitcher throw to only four or five batters. Then have another hurler or player throw to the remaining hitters.

- Pitching strategy varies. Here's a simple plan: Have the pitcher throw straight balls for two minutes, a mixture of straight and breaking pitches for two minutes, and breaking pitches only for the last minute.

- The coach keeps time. After five minutes, athletes rotate— Station 9 to Station 1, Station 1 to Station 2, Station 2 to Station 3, and so on. After Team A hits, change sides. Group A takes the field; Group B comes to bat and goes through the stations.

Comments: The drill may accommodate a larger number of players, but it works best with 14 to 18 athletes. Every player has something to do and the coach stays busy helping athletes with hitting and fielding problems. Remind fungo batters to stay alert and hit balls between pitches, not when the hitter is swinging at a ball. Make certain batters wear protective helmets. Keep players hustling. Too much delay lengthens the drill.

56 FIVE-MINUTE HIT/FIVE-MINUTE BUNT

Objective: To combine hitting, bunting, and fielding.
Location: Baseball diamond.
Technique: Athletes practice hitting, bunting, and fielding skills.

Procedure: Have athletes do the following—

- Repeat Drill 55, Five-Minute Hit. Make the following change: Substitute Station 2, on-deck batter, with live pitch bunting. Move Station 2 from behind the batting cage to the right sideline fence near first base.

- A player, acting as pitcher, stands about 30 feet away and faces the batter. The batter concentrates on bunting the ball to the left, to the right, and back to the pitcher.

Comments: See Drill 55, Five-Minute Hit.

57 THREE-INNING HITTING GAME

Objective: To combine hitting, bunting, and fielding.
Location: Baseball diamond.
Technique: Athletes work on their stance, stride, and swing.

Procedure: Have athletes do the following—

- Divide the team into Groups A and B, with nine players (optional) per group. Group A, the offense, comes to home plate. Group B, the defense, takes the field. Game rules are as follows:

  1. Each player on the offensive team comes to bat three times per inning. He receives three swings or three chances to hit the ball.

  2. He runs out every hit. He may reach base safely on hits, errors, walks, catcher's interference, or when struck by a pitched ball.

  3. A runner may advance on errors, hits, walks, sacrifice flies, bunts, passed balls, wild pitches, catcher's interference, or when the pitcher hits the batter. NOTE: Do not

let runners steal or pitchers give intentional walks. Allow runners to lead off from base.

4. If a runner or batter makes an out, he returns to the end of the line and bats in turn.

5. A batter walks when the pitcher fails to throw a strike on two consecutive pitches.

6. A hitter strikes out when he takes a called strike or fouls a pitch.

7. Runners clear the bases after three outs. Sides change when the last hitter completes his third time at bat. Athletes rotate. Group B comes to bat; Group A takes the field.

8. The pitcher throws at one-half to three-quarter speed.

9. The game lasts three innings. Each team keeps track of its own score. The team with the most runs wins. Regardless of score, both teams complete their time at bat.

Comments: Have extra players work in small groups or umpire until they enter the game. Make sure hitters and runners wear protective helmets. Remind catchers to wear full protective gear. Urge offensive and defensive players to try various game strategies. Keep athletes hustling on and off the field.

58 STAY AT THE PLATE

Objective: To combine hitting, bunting, and fielding.
Location: Baseball diamond.
Technique: Athletes practice hitting, bunting, and fielding skills.

Procedure: Have athletes do the following—

- Divide the team into Groups A and B, with nine players (optional) per group. Group A, offense, comes to home plate. Group B, defense, takes the field.

- Group A athletes alternate hitting and bunting. For example, Player 1 swings away, Player 2 bunts, Player 3 swings away, Player 4 bunts, and so on. Each athlete receives four chances per round to hit and bunt. After one round teams change sides. Group A takes the field; Group B comes to bat.

Give athletes these guidelines:

- The batter stays at the plate until he hits or bunts the ball into fair territory. He must run out each hit or bunt.
- Regular baseball rules apply. Exceptions: Batters do not walk. They cannot take first on catcher's interference or when struck by a pitched ball. Allow runners to lead off from base and steal.
- The pitcher throws at one-half to three-quarter speed.
- If a runner or batter makes an out, he returns to the end of the line and bats in turn.
- Runners clear the bases after three outs. Regardless of number of outs, teams change sides after one round. Each team bats for three rounds.
- Teams keep track of their own scores. Let the losing team run laps, do push-ups, or put away equipment.

Comments: See Comments, Drill 57, Three-Inning Hitting Game. SUGGESTION: Keep offensive athletes busy. Have them swing a weighted bat or hit off the tee until they come to the plate.

59 LAST INNING

Objective: To stress scoring the winning run.
Location: Baseball diamond.
Technique: Two teams (A and B) have three outs in which to score runs. They can execute any play they wish.

Procedure: Have athletes do the following—

- Near the end of practice pick two evenly divided teams. Team A goes on offense; Team B plays defense.
- Situation: It's the last inning and the score is tied, 1 to 1. Each team has three outs in which to score the winning run(s). If at the end of the inning the score remains tied, both teams run three laps around the track. If a team scores the winning run(s), the losing team runs two laps around the track.
- Players must bat in order. Any team caught cheating automatically loses.

Comments: Players enjoy this drill before ending practice. It gives them something to look forward to. Teams should start where they left off the day before, for instance, if the fifth batter made the last out, the sixth hitter leads off the new drill. If possible keep the same teams.

60 THREE-TEAM SWING

Objective: To stress basic hitting fundamentals.
Location: Baseball field.
Technique: Each team spends 20 minutes hitting off the batting tee and 40 minutes hitting live pitching.

Figure 4–1
Three-Team Swing

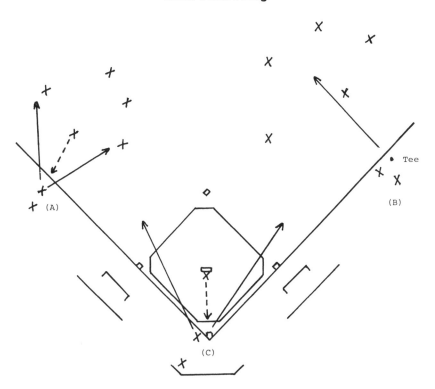

Procedure: Have athletes do the following—

- Divide players evenly into three groups. Each group (A, B, and C) goes to a different station. After 20 minutes they change, moving in a clockwise direction. **(See Figure 4–1.)**
- Set up and locate the stations as follows:
    - Station 1   Hitting live pitching   left field foul line
    - Station 2   Hitting off the batting tee   right field foul line
    - Station 3   Hitting live pitching   home plate

Comments: Players need to stay alert since baseballs come from various directions. Athletes are responsible for shagging their own group's balls. Station 1 requires a back-up man to shag passed balls or foul tips. All balls must be returned quickly to prevent wasting valuable time. If a small portable screen or net is available, place it directly behind the hitter. At the live pitching stations hitters should stress meeting the ball squarely out in front of home plate. Home-run hitting is not desirable at these locations. Allow each player a two-swing minimum per time at bat.

61 BACKSTOP AND BATTING CAGE

Objective: To increase the number of swings per batting session.
Location: Baseball diamond.
Technique: Two batters hit at the same time and in different directions. Each player receives 20 to 30 swings per session.

Procedure: Have athletes do the following—

- Move the batting cage between the backstop and home plate, approximately 10 feet from the backstop. Divide players into equal groups. Group A hits and fields between second and third base foul area; Group B hits and fields between second and first base foul area. **(See Figure 4–2.)**
- Group A pitcher throws from the third base foul line, standing between third and home; Group B pitcher throws from the first base foul line, standing between first and home.
- Each player receives 10 swings per turn at bat. Every player goes around at least three times. Left-handed hitters should be in Group A. Pitchers should change often.

Figure 4–2
Backstop and Batting Cage

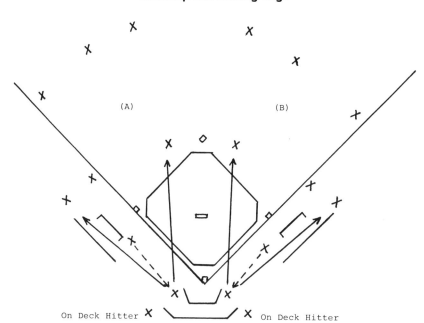

Comments: This is an excellent activity for coach and players. Players receive plenty of hitting practice and the coach can help those hitters experiencing difficulty.

62 ROTATING TEAMS

Objective: To provide an interesting, fast-moving batting practice.
Location: Baseball diamond.
Technique: Three teams alternate between hitting and fielding.

Procedure: Have athletes do the following—

- Select three teams from the regular squad. One team (Team A) is at bat while the remaining two teams (B and C) are evenly distributed in the field.
- If more than nine players are in the field, place half the players between first and second base while the remaining half stay between second and third base.

- Each unit or team receives three rotations or rounds in which to bat and score runs. Each rotation allows every player five different chances to hit the ball. Only hypothetical baserunners are used. Each hit, regardless of length, is considered a single as far as advancing the players is concerned.

- Each team comes to bat three times. Each player receives a minimum of 15 swings. After each batter on Team A completes his turn, Team A goes into the field; then Team B comes to bat. After Team B finishes its turn at bat, Team C comes to the plate.

- The number of innings per rotation may vary due to the number of players per side and conditions affecting the outs. The number of times a player comes to bat remains the same since each man is at bat five times per rotation or 15 times for three rotations. The last man up in the roster or lineup always receives his turn at bat, even if the third out occurs previously in the inning. This guarantees every player a minimum of 15 times at bat. Each team's inning consists of three outs regulated by the following conditions:

    1. No actual runners are used. Fictitious runners are used when conditions or situations call for them.

    2. Each batter receives one swing. If he makes a base hit, he continues swinging until he either misses the ball, takes a called strike, fouls the pitch, or makes a routine out (error included). Each base hit entitles the batter to an extra swing. He continues to swing until he fails to make a base hit.

    3. Fly balls, ground balls, forceouts, and strikeouts make up routine outs.

    4. The catcher may be used to call all balls and strikes and judge all batted balls (hits and errors).

    5. If the pitch hits the dirt, goes over the batter's head, or stays out of the strike zone and the batter swings, it is recorded as an out unless the pitch is connected for a base hit, for example.

    6. Passed balls or wild pitches go as ball counts but not as base advancements for any runner.

    7. Bases on balls are issued and runners may advance; however, the batter remains at home plate and a new count begins.

8. If the pitch strikes the batter, a runner is placed at first. The batter stays at home plate and a new count is started. All runners advance one base.

9. The batter does not receive extra swings in case of error situations.

10. Runners advance one base on any type of base hit. This rule can be changed subject to the number of players or the field conditions.

11. Force plays are easily made in the field, but trying to determine double-play situations only leads to trouble. Without actual runners, a simple force play will alleviate many problems and save a great deal of bickering.

12. Tag-ups on fly balls are not allowed since there is no logical way of telling whether a runner would have been safe or out.

13. All situations requiring runner advancement tax the thinking ability of each player since actual runners are not used. Decisions are made with imagination and from previous experience in similar circumstances.

Comments: The coach should use available pitchers or players with good control to speed up the drill and keep it interesting. Pitchers should mix their pitches. This keeps the drill on a gamelike basis and offers an opportunity for batter concentration. Varsity pitchers working against junior varsity players also works well in this drill.

It is possible for each team to score runs through hits, errors, walks, or being hit by the pitch. Making a game of it adds zest to the practice and increases the player's interest level. If the teams stay evenly balanced, scores will be very close with many ties prevailing.

Playing both defense and offense, players develop a sense of competition through this gamelike drill while developing the necessary skills in baseball. This can be enhanced further by providing two or three laps around the track after practice for the two losing teams.

THE BUNTER

Players often neglect spending enough time on bunting practice. Some athletes feel bunting is less important than hitting because they are seldom called upon to bunt. The coach's attitude plays a big part in getting players to work on their bunting. If he believes bunting is important, he must convince his athletes by offering bunting drills in practice. A simple philosophy is score one run at a time; use the bunt to get men into scoring position.

The following drills and games will help the player improve his bunting skills.

63 DROP IT GAME

Objective: To practice bunting the ball.

Location: Backstop or fence areas.

Technique: Bunters concentrate on watching the ball hit the bat, holding the bat level, and laying the ball on the ground.

Procedure: Have athletes do the following—

- Divide players into groups of four and send groups near the backstop or fence. Each group brings balls, gloves, and bats with them. Player 2, pitcher, stands about 40 feet away from Player 1, hitter. Player 3, fielder, stays to the right of Player 2. Player 4, fielder, stays to the left of Player 2. Rags or towels make suitable base lines.

- Action begins when the pitcher, throwing at half speed, delivers a ball to the hitter. The batter bunts the ball down either base line. He receives one point if the ball stays in fair territory. If he pops up, fouls, or misses the pitch, he receives no points. The hitter keeps track of his points.

- After six chances the athletes rotate. Player 1 becomes Player 2, Player 2 becomes Player 3, Player 3 becomes Player 4, and Player 4 becomes Player 1. Each athlete comes to bat twice. The pitcher throws at three-quarter speed during the second round. The athlete earning the most points wins.

Comments: Circulate among the groups and offer help to those having trouble. Keep a lookout for these problems:

- Failure to hold bat level. The player who tilts or drops the end of his bat is likely to foul off the pitch.

- Bat held too close to body. The batter doesn't get a good look at the ball. He will likely foul off many pitches. The hitter should hold the bat well out in front of home plate.

- Hitter pulls the bat back. The batter should hold his arms straight until he bunts the ball. NOTE: A successful bunter crouches slightly and flexes his arms at the elbow.

- Hitter turns and faces the pitcher too soon. A smart pitcher, with men on base, will attempt a fake pick-off to see if the batter intends to bunt. A batter gives himself away by dropping the bat head or sliding his hands up the bat handle. The hitter should shift to a bunting position just before the pitcher releases the ball. Exception: The hitter waits until the ball leaves the pitcher's hand before squaring around on a suicide squeeze play.

- Batter bunts the ball too hard. The hitter is probably gripping the bat too tightly with his upper hand. The bat should rest lightly between the thumb and fingers.

- Hitter bunts too many balls foul. Check his body position in the batter's box. He may be standing back too far. Move him into the front part of the batter's box. NOTE: Have players try the pivot position and square around position. Let them select which foot position works best for them.

64 SACRIFICE SCORE GAME

Objective: To practice bunting the ball.
Location: Backstop or fence areas.
Technique: Bunters concentrate on watching the ball hit the bat, holding the bat level, and laying the ball on the ground.

Procedure: Have athletes do the following—

- Divide players into groups of four. Send groups near the backstop or fence. Each group brings balls, gloves, bats, and old towels or rags for bases. (If available, use rubber bases.) Each group sets up a diamond with bases approximately 60 feet apart and pitcher's mound about 40 feet away from home plate. Fielders stay to the left, to the right, and behind the pitcher.

- Action begins when two groups meet. Group 1, offense, comes to home plate. Group 2, defense, takes the field. Game rules are as follows:

1. The pitcher throws at three-quarter speed. Do not allow hurler to lob the ball. Slow pitching throws off a batter's timing.

2. The offensive team bunts for 10 minutes. Batters must hit in turn. For example, if bases are loaded and the fourth hitter strikes out, the first batter must leave third base, come to home plate, and hit.

3. The batter stays at home plate until he bunts the ball or makes an out. He runs out balls bunted into fair territory.

4. A player makes an out when he pops up, fouls, or misses the pitch.

5. Runners may slide. They cannot lead off or steal. Player 1, pitcher, is the only player allowed to field bunts. Players 2, 3, and 4 must stay near their bases. Their job is to tag out runners.

6. Let defensive players change positions whenever they wish. Switching positions keeps the drill interesting.

7. The pitcher makes put-outs at home plate. He must tag out the runner.

8. Runners clear the bases after three outs. Teams keep track of their own score. The team with the most runs after two rounds wins.

9. Sides change after 10 minutes. Group 1 takes the field; Group 2 comes to bat.

Comments: Remind athletes that runners cannot leave base until the batter bunts the ball. If a runner leaves too soon, he's out, and must return to the end of the line. Make sure batters and runners wear protective equipment.

65 PARTNER BUNT GAME

Objective: To practice bunting the ball.
Location: Backstop or fence area.
Technique: Bunters concentrate on watching the ball hit the bat, holding the bat level, and laying the ball on the ground.

Procedure: Have athletes do the following—

• Divide players into groups of three. Send groups near the backstop or fence. Each group brings balls, gloves, bats, and a rubber base for first base.

- Action begins when two groups meet. Group 1, offense, comes to home plate. Group 2, defense, positions itself in the following manner: Player 1, pitcher, stands about 40 feet away from the hitter. Player 2, fielder, stays to the right of the pitcher. Player 3, fielder, stays to the left of the pitcher. First base is about 70 feet from home plate.
- Game rules are as follows:
  1. The pitcher throws at three-quarter speed. He concentrates on throwing strikes.
  2. The offensive team bunts for 10 minutes. Hitters bunt in order and must run out every ball bunted in fair territory.
  3. When a player reaches first safely, he must stay there until a teammate bunts him home. If his teammate fails, his teammate is out, and goes to the end of the line and bats in turn.
  4. Defensive players cannot move until the batter bunts the ball.
  5. A player makes an out when he pops up, fouls, or misses the pitch.
  6. Do not allow runners to lead off.
  7. Player 3 acts as first baseman. Player 2 or the pitcher covers home plate. The runner must be tagged out at home.
  8. After three outs, the runner leaves first base.
  9. Each team keeps its own score. The team scoring the most runs wins.
  10. Sides change after 10 minutes. Group 1 takes the field; Group 2 comes to bat. Go for two rounds.

Comments: Make sure batters and runners wear protective equipment.

66 SQUEEZE 'EM IN

Objective: To practice bringing across the tying or winning run.
Location: Baseball diamond.
Technique: The two main types of squeeze bunts—suicide and delayed—require many hours of practice to perfect. The suicide squeeze is the most dangerous. If the batter isn't a reliable bunter,

the runner is stopped cold from scoring. The safety squeeze is less daring. The batter bunts only good pitches (strikes) and the runner, usually a fast man, streaks for home only after the batter lays the ball down in fair territory.

Procedure: Have athletes do the following—

- Pitcher, runners, catcher, third and first basemen take their positions. The remaining players receive one pitch to bunt. Fielders make plays on all balls and batters run out each bunt. The coach makes periodic fielding changes.
- Runners line up near the third base coaching box. Play begins when the pitcher winds up, a runner leads off from third base, and the batter turns to bunt the pitch. The coach, standing behind the pitcher, yells out either "Suicide" or "Safety." The batter, fielders, and runner react accordingly.
- Squeeze 'Em In, a point game, scores as follows:

Situation	Points
Runner scores.	2
The batter misses or fouls the pitch.	0
Runner is out.	− 1

- The player receiving the most points wins.

Comments: If a pitcher catches a runner leaving early from third base, he should throw a tough pitch to bunt, such as, high and outside for left-handed hitters; high and inside for right-handed hitters.

INCLEMENT WEATHER ACTIVITIES

Here are three indoor activities for hitters during inclement weather.

67 THREE PITCH

Objective: Athletes practice fundamental skills necessary for successful team play. Players work on both offensive and defensive strategy.
Location: Gymnasium.
Technique: Players concentrate on running, fielding, and hitting skills.

Procedure: Have athletes do the following—

- Set up a baseball diamond. Use movable rubber bases.
- Select two full teams, nine players per team.
- Play begins when the defense, Team A, takes the field. The catcher wears full protective equipment. The offense, Team B, sends a man to first base. A batter comes to the plate. He takes three pitches. Each pitch presents a different situation. They are as follows:

—Situation 1, first pitch—	The batter has a 3–1 count; he must hit-and-run on the <u>first</u> pitch.
—Situation 2, second pitch—	The hitter must bunt the <u>second</u> pitch.
—Situation 3, third pitch—	The hitter can bunt or swing away on the <u>third</u> pitch. (Batters should use a smooth, easy swing with a complete follow-through.) Hitters run out the last swing.

- A batter makes an out if he swings and misses on any pitch, fouls the pitch, or takes a called strike. He reaches base on walks (pitcher misses on all three deliveries), catcher's interference, errors, being hit by the pitch, or base hits. The batter runs out only the third pitch. Runners, however, go every time the batter hits the ball.
- Runners advance on base hits, errors, wild pitches, tag-ups, or passed balls. No stealing is allowed (Exception: hit-and-run).
- Every player bats twice each inning. The pitcher throws a tennis or rubber ball to 18 batters.
- After three outs, runners leave the bases and return to the end of the line. Another player goes to first base and play continues. After every hitter bats twice, sides change regardless of number of outs. Team B takes the field; Team A comes to bat.
- The catcher (designated player or coach) umpires the game.
- Caution pitchers to throw at half-speed; warn runners not to slide or interfere with play. The team scoring the most runs wins.

Comments: The coach may wish to demonstrate any of the following skills prior to the drill:

- How to hit behind the runner
- Proper bunting techniques
- Rundowns
- Hitting the ball up the middle of the diamond
- Base running tips, such as leading off base, getting the jump on the pitcher, and so forth

68 PLACE HIT

Objective: To practice hitting and fielding skills.
Location: Gymnasium.
Technique: Athletes concentrate on place hitting the pitched ball.

Procedure: Have all athletes do the following—

- Divide team into three or four groups with four players per group. Send each group to a different area of the gymnasium.
- Player A, batter, stands near the gym wall; Player B, pitcher, stays approximately 50 feet away facing Player A. Players C and D, fielders, remain close together behind the pitcher. Player C stands to the right of Player B; Player D keeps to the left of Player B.
- Action begins when Player B pitches a tennis or rubber ball to Player A. Player C breaks to his right; Player D runs about 40 feet to his left. The batter, using a choke grip, taps the ball toward Player C. Player C fields and throws the ball to Player D. Player D returns the ball to Player B.
- Player A receives two pitches. He hits the first delivery to Player C; he hits the second pitch to Player D.
- Players rotate clockwise, then Player A becomes Player C; Player C becomes Player B; Player B becomes Player D; and Player D becomes the hitter.
- Award points as follows:

  2 points   The fielder makes a clean play, including a good throw.

  1 point   The batter hits the ball to the correct fielder.

> 0 points   A batter receives no points if he does the following: Hits a ball the fielder cannot reach; hits a pitch to the wrong fielder; or misses or fouls the pitch.
> A fielder receives no points if he bobbles or throws the ball wildly.

- The first player earning 10 points wins.

Comments: Every player has a chance to throw, field, and hit the ball. Changing positions often keeps players interested. Most athletes react positively to a program which offers variety, including fast-moving drills.

69 BUNT ONE

Objective: A six-inning game designed to score runs.
Location: Gymnasium.
Technique: Players work on their running, fielding, and hitting skills.

Procedure: Have athletes do the following—

- Set up a baseball diamond. Use movable rubber bases.
- Select two teams of infielders with six players per team.
- Play begins when the defense, Team A, takes the field. The catcher wears full protective equipment. The offense, Team B, sends a man to first base. A batter comes to the plate. Objective: To score runs; it's the hitter's job to advance the runner.
- The batter receives two pitches per time at bat; he must bunt one of the pitches. Every player bats twice each inning. If the batter fails to bunt the ball into fair territory, he's out; he returns to the end of the line.
- The hurler throws a tennis or rubber ball to 12 batters each inning. If the pitcher fails to throw strikes or hits the batter, the batter is awarded first base. The next man in line comes to the plate.
- After three outs, runners leave the base and return to the end of the line. After every hitter bats twice, sides change regardless of number of outs—Team B takes the field; Team A comes to bat.

- Runners advance on walks, tag-ups, wild pitches, passed balls, errors, bunts—or steals (if it's part of the offensive strategy).
- Runners leave the bases after three outs. Another player goes to first base and play continues. Caution runners not to slide or interfere with play.
- The catcher (designated player or coach) umpires the game.
- The game lasts six innings. The coach makes necessary substitutions.
- The team scoring the most runs in six innings wins. Extra laps or push-ups for the losing players add interest to the game.

Comments: The coach makes defensive and offensive changes. The offensive team, by using prearranged signals, can execute several plays: suicide or safety squeeze, run and bunt, fake bunt and run, etc. Infielders have an opportunity to practice defensive strategy: base coverage, forceouts, rundowns, stopping the squeeze, and so forth. The coach must be sure that all players stay busy and that athletes play their normal positions. Extra players can work individual or small group drills until the coach calls for them.

chapter five

Drills and Games for the Entire Team

Athletes respond well to challenging activities. This chapter includes competitive games that cover hitting, bunting, fielding, and base-running skills.

The following 10 suggestions will help the games run smoothly:

- Divide athletes into two teams with nine players per team.

- Give the offensive team two choices: Let the players decide in which order they wish to hit, or have them bat according to player number, e.g., pitcher first, catcher second, first baseman third, and so forth.

- Tell pitchers to throw at three-quarter speed. Have them mix their pitches. In most of these drills the pitcher's control is the key to success. A wild thrower slows down the action and players will soon lose interest. Make sure hurlers warm their arms properly.

- Have pitchers throw from the stretch with men on base.

- Limit hurlers to four or five warm-up pitches. Too much throwing between rounds prolongs the game.

- Have catchers wear full protective gear, such as, cup, shin guards, chest protector, and mask. Exception: When the catcher plays roving fielder this is not necessary.
- Let the manager or catcher handle umpiring chores.
- Each team keeps its score. The team with the most points wins. Have the losing squad run laps or do push-ups.
- Let athletes experiment. Urge them to try different offensive and defensive strategies.
- Caution players to wear protective helmets, sliding pads, and long-legged pants.

70 THREE CUTS

Objective: To practice hitting, bunting, base-running, and fielding.
Location: Baseball diamond.
Technique: To concentrate on strengthening the skills necessary for successful team play.

Procedure: Have athletes do the following—

- The defensive team takes the field. The offensive team lines up near home plate.
- Each batter receives three swings per round. A round consists of nine players coming to bat. The hitter is free to bunt or hit any pitch.
- If the batter hits a ball on the third swing into fair territory, he runs it out. NOTE: The hitter does not run out the first or second hit when runners are on base.
- Rule: At least one player must reach first base during the first round of hitting (nine batters). If no one reaches first base, the sides change, and the defensive team comes to bat. NOTE: This rule does not apply to Rounds 2, 3, or 4.
- Runners advance on errors, hits, walks, sacrifice flies, bunts, passed balls (third strike), wild pitches, catcher's interference, or when the pitcher hits the batter. NOTE: Do not allow intentional walks.
- A batter retires when he strikes out, fouls out, flies out, or grounds out on the third swing. He returns to the end of the line and hits in regular order.

- A player strikes out when he takes a third strike or fouls the third swing.
- A batter walks when the pitcher fails to throw a strike on two consecutive pitches.
- Rule: A hitter cannot advance beyond first base on extra base hits. For example, if the batter hits the ball over the fence he must stop at first. However, runners may score from second and third. A runner on first cannot go past third.
- Do not record the number of outs. Athletes continue to hit until sides change.
- The hitter receives three swings in his attempt to score runner(s). For example, the batter hits the first pitch for a single, sending a runner to third. He has two more chances to knock in his teammate(s). If the hitter fails to score the runner(s), the runner(s) must leave the base, return to the line, and hit in regular order.
- If there are no runners on base and the batter hits the pitch, he must run the ball out.
- A runner may lead off base; he cannot steal.
- Each team hits for two rounds (optional). After two rounds, sides change. Exception: If no player reaches first base in the first round, sides change.

Comments: A coach who umpires behind the pitcher's mound can make necessary adjustments and keep the game moving at a constant pace.

71 THREE PITCH/TWO SWING

Objective: To practice hitting, bunting, base-running, and fielding.
Location: Baseball diamond.
Technique: To concentrate on strengthening the skills necessary for successful team play.

Procedure: Have athletes do the following—

- The defensive team takes the field. The offensive team lines up near home plate.
- The batter receives three pitches. He gets two chances or two swings to hit the ball.

- The batter is free to bunt or swing away. If he hits the first pitch, he must run it out.
- An athlete strikes out when he swings through or fouls the second pitch, or takes the second pitch for a strike.
- A batter retires when he strikes out, fouls out, flies out, or grounds out. He returns to the line and hits in regular order.
- Runners advance on errors, hits, walks, sacrifice flies, bunts, passed balls (second strike), wild pitches, catcher's interference, or when the pitcher hits the batter. NOTE: Do not allow intentional walks.
- When a runner makes an out, he returns to the line and hits in regular order.
- Runners, unless thrown out or tagged out, must remain on base until they score. Allow runners to steal.
- Each team bats for 10 minutes. After that time runners clear the bases and the offensive team takes the field. The defensive team comes to bat. Do not record the number of outs. Athletes continue to hit until sides change. Players keep their hitting order. For example, if the shortstop makes the last out, the left fielder bats when his team hits again. NOTE: Teams decide ahead of time which batting order to use.
- A round lasts approximately 20 minutes. The game consists of three rounds (optional).

Comments: See Drill 70, Three Cuts.

72 TWO LIVE/TWO FUNGO

Objective: To practice hitting, bunting, base-running, and fielding.
Location: Baseball diamond.
Technique: To concentrate on strengthening the skills necessary for successful team play.

Procedure: Have athletes do the following—

- The defensive team takes the field. The offensive team lines up near home plate. They bring a fungo bat and ball with them.
- Batters alternate swinging at the pitcher's delivery and hitting the ball with a fungo bat. For example, Batter 1 receives two swings to hit the pitched ball. If he hits the ball into fair

territory, he runs it out. Batter 2 comes to home plate with fungo bat and ball. The hurler delivers a pitch to the catcher. When the pitch hits the catcher's mitt, the batter fungos his ball and runs it out. NOTE: The batter does not swing at the pitched ball. Play continues with Batter 3 hitting a live pitch, Batter 4 hitting a fungo, and so forth.

- Runners advance on errors, hits, walks, sacrifice flies, bunts, passed balls (first strike), wild pitches, catcher's interference, or when the pitcher hits the batter. NOTE: Do not allow stealing when a batter fungos the ball.
- The hitter may bunt the live pitch and fungo bunt the ball. Rule: A batter may fungo the ball between the outfielders. He's not allowed to hit the ball over an outfielder's head.
- An athlete strikes out when he takes a second strike, fouls the ball on his second swing, or swings and misses on his second attempt. The fungo batter strikes out when he fouls the ball or swings and misses.
- A batter retires when he strikes out, fouls out, pops out, grounds out, or if he is a fungo batter and hits the ball over an outfielder's head. He returns to the line and hits in regular order.
- A batter walks when the pitcher fails to throw a strike on two consecutive pitches.
- After three outs, runners clear the bases, return to the line, and hit in regular order.
- Each player hits four times (two live/two fungo) in one round before changing places with the defensive team. Regardless of the number of outs, the sides change. The game consists of two rounds (optional).

Comments: See Drill 70, Three Cuts.

73 SIMPLY FUNGO

Objective: To practice base-running, fielding, and hitting with the fungo bat.
Location: Baseball diamond.
Technique: To concentrate on strengthening the skills necessary for successful team play.

Procedure: Have athletes do the following—

- The defensive team takes the field. The offensive team lines up near home plate. They keep a fungo bat and ball with them.
- Each batter, in turn, fungos a ball somewhere in the field. Rule: A batter is not allowed to hit a ball over an outfielder's head. If he does, he's out. However, the batter can place a ball between the outfielders.
- The athlete runs out every hit. A batter retires when he fouls the ball, swings and misses, grounds out, pops out, flies out, or hits the ball over an outfielder's head. He returns to the line and hits in regular order.
- Runners advance on errors, hits, sacrifice flies and bunts. They can lead off from base, but cannot steal.
- After three outs, runners clear the bases, return to the line, and hit in regular order.
- Each player hits two times in one round. After the last player hits, the sides change. Players switch regardless of number of outs. The game consists of three rounds (optional).

Comments: See Drill 70, Three Cuts.

74 ONE CHANCE

Objective: To practice hitting, bunting, base-running, and fielding.
Location: Baseball diamond.
Technique: To concentrate on strengthening the skills necessary for successful team play.

Procedure: Have athletes do the following—

- The defensive team takes the field. The offensive team lines up near home plate.
- Each batter receives one pitch. If he hits the ball into fair territory, he runs to first base. If he makes an out, the batter returns to the line and hits in regular order.
- A batter retires when he strikes out, grounds out, pops out, or flies out.
- Regular baseball rules apply. Runners advance on hits, walks, errors, wild pitches, passed balls, sacrifice flies and bunts. NOTE: Do not allow intentional walks.

- Players can lead off from base and steal.
- A batter may bunt or swing away. A hitter strikes out when he swings and misses, or takes a called strike.
- The batter walks when the pitcher fails to throw a strike.
- After three outs, runners clear the bases, return to the line, and hit in regular order.
- Each player hits three times in one round. After the last player hits, sides change. Players switch regardless of number of outs. The game consists of three rounds (optional).

Comments: See Drill 70, Three Cuts.

75 TWO POP

Objective: To practice hitting, bunting, base-running, and fielding.
Location: Baseball diamond.
Technique: To concentrate on strengthening the skills necessary for successful team play.

Procedure: Have athletes do the following—

- The defensive team takes the field. The offensive team lines up near home plate.
- The offensive team forms two lines. Five players go to Line A and four players go to Line B. Line A athletes act as hitters; they line up to the left of the batting cage. Line B players represent runners; they line up to the right of the batting cage.
- Action begins when Player 1, Line A, comes to bat. He has two chances or two swings to hit the ball. If he hits the ball into fair territory, Player 1, Line B, runs the ball out. If Player 1, Line B, makes an out, he goes to the end of Line A. Player 1, Line A, goes to the end of Line B.
- The hitter receives two swings. He may bunt or swing at the pitch. An athlete strikes out when he takes a second strike, fouls the ball on his second swing, or swings and misses on his second attempt.
- A batter retires when he strikes out, pops out, flies out, or grounds out. He goes to Line B and becomes a runner.
- Runners advance on errors, hits, walks, sacrifice flies, bunts, passed balls (second strike), wild pitches, catcher's

interference, or when the pitcher hits the batter. NOTE: Do not allow intentional walks. Allow runners to steal.

- A batter walks when the pitcher builds a three-ball count. For example, the hurler runs a two-ball, one-strike count on the batter. If the pitcher's next delivery misses the strike zone, the batter walks.

- Each team bats for 15 minutes. After that time, runners clear the bases and the offensive team takes the field. The defensive team comes to bat. Do not record the number of outs. Athletes continue to hit until sides change. Players keep their hitting order.

- A round lasts for 30 minutes. A round allows each team to field for 15 minutes and hit for 15 minutes. The game consists of two rounds (optional).

Comments: See Drill 70, Three Cuts.

76 LIVE BATTER

Objective: To strengthen team defensive skills.
Location: Baseball diamond.
Technique: Players practice fielding, throwing, and backing up.

Procedure: Have athletes do the following—

- Players take their regular positions. Runners (extra players and pitchers) line up behind or to one side of the backstop and take turns hitting. Each player runs out every swing, hit, or miss.

- Each runner receives only one pitch. If he fails to make contact, he runs toward first base when the ball hits the catcher's glove. Other runners advance at their own risk.

- The coach stands in the third base coaching box and gives signals to the hitters. These prearranged signs keep the offensive and defensive players alert.

- Vary the number of outs. Switch from 2 to 3, 4, 6, or 9 outs. Players take a greater interest when the procedure changes frequently.

Comments: Change practice-ending activities often to hold player interest. Include the Live Batter drill at least once every two weeks.

77 COACH CALLS IT

Objective: To strengthen team defensive skills.
Location: Baseball diamond.
Technique: Players practice fielding, throwing, and backing up.

Procedure: Have athletes do the following—

- Players take their regular positions. Runners line up at home plate. The coach assigns runners to different bases, that is, first and second, second and third, third only, etc.
- The coach calls out a situation. For example, he says, "Fourth inning. You're behind 1 to 0. There's one out with a man on second. A real good hitter is up." The team adjusts accordingly.
- The pitcher winds up and throws the ball to the catcher. The coach hits the ball however and wherever he chooses.

Comments: A fair-hitting coach adds flavor to the drill. He mixes pop flies, high bounders, and line drives with drag bunts and intentional misses. A daydreaming third baseman suddenly awakes when a fake bunt turns into a "hair-parting" line drive.

Simulating game conditions provides a comfortable atmosphere for learning. A wise coach uses every spare moment to teach correct defensive strategy to his charges.

78 FOUR STATIONS

Objective: To offer players a change from regular practice.
Location: Baseball diamond.
Technique: Players travel to four stations and practice base-running, hitting, bunting, and ball-tossing accuracy.

Procedure: Have athletes do the following—

- Divide athletes into four teams, with four or five players (optional) per team. Set up four stations around the baseball field.
- Action begins when each team goes to a different station and performs the scheduled activity. The procedure for each station is as follows:

–Station 1 (Location: Home plate)

Each player in turn brings a bat to home plate and assumes his normal stance. Another athlete, holding a timer, yells "Go." The player swings the bat and runs to first. His time is recorded on a card (Card 1). Repeat the procedure twice. Have players time one another from home plate to second base and all the way around the bases. Tell them to average the three times and record them on the scoring card.

STATION 1: SCORING CARD

| Player | Home to First | STATION 1 | | Average Time | Points |
		Home to Second	Circle Bases		

–Station 2 (Location: Left field)

Place a glove in deep center field. Have players take turns hitting a fungo ball to the glove. Another athlete, standing by the glove, measures the distance between the ball and glove. The distance is recorded on a card (Card 2). Athletes receive two fungos. Have them average the two measurements and record on the scoring card.

STATION 2: SCORING CARD

STATION 2				
Player	Fungo One	Fungo Two	Average Distance	Points

–Station 3 (Location: Right field, near sideline fence)

Athletes spread out as follows: Player 1, pitcher, stands about 40 feet in front of the baseline fence. He throws at one-half speed to Player 2, the batter. Player 2 stands next to the fence and faces Player 1. Players 3, 4, and 5, fielders, stay to the left and to the right of Player 1. Use old towels or rags for baselines.

The batter receives three chances to bunt the ball. Players 3, 4, or 5 measure the distance between the ball and baseline target with a tape measure. Have them average the three measurements and record on the scoring card (Card 3).

STATION 3: SCORING CARD

STATION 3					
Player	Bunt One	Bunt Two	Bunt Three	Avg. Distance	Points

–Station 4 (Location: Between first base and the backstop)
Place a glove approximately 150 feet away from the group.
A player stands near the glove. Another athlete, standing 150
feet away, makes an underhand toss toward the glove. The
athlete continues to toss or roll the ball until it lands in the
pocket of the glove. The number of rolls or tosses are recorded
on a card (Card 4). Athletes repeat the procedure two times.
Have them average the number of tosses for both trials and
record on the scoring card.

STATION 4: SCORING CARD

Player	STATION 4		Avg. Number of Tosses	Points
	Toss One	Toss Two		

Give athletes these rules for each station:

- Station 1

    –If a player misses a base or fails to hustle (as judged by his
    teammates), he comes in last.
    –Require athletes to take a full cut. Start timing when the bat
    hits the ground.

- Station 2

    –Allow each player one swing per fungo.
    –If a player misses or fouls the ball, he receives a score of 150
    feet.

- Station 3

    –Count only balls bunted into fair territory.
    –Do not penalize batter for pitches fouled or missed.

- Station 4

    –Athlete must release ball from a point between the shoul-
    ders and knees.
    –A player cannot pick up the ball until it stops rolling.

Comments: The coach keeps time. He gives each group 15 minutes to complete the activity. After that time, athletes move to the next station. Players like to improve their scores; sometimes this leads to confusion. Avoid problems by not letting athletes keep their own scores. Have them exchange cards and rely on each other's honesty.

Hold a preliminary meeting. Pass out four score cards per player (3 x 5 index cards) and pencils. NOTE: Save time—make up cards ahead of time. Explain the rules and how to keep score. Have athletes award points in this manner: 10 points for first place; 7 points for second place; 5 points for third place; 3 points for fourth place; 1 point for fifth place.

79 THREE STATIONS

Objective: To offer players a change from regular practice.
Location: Baseball diamond.
Technique: To practice making accurate throws and hitting with a fungo bat.

Procedure: Have athletes do the following—

- Divide athletes into three teams, with six or seven players (optional) per team. Set up three stations around the baseball field.

- Action begins when each team goes to a different station and performs the scheduled activity. The procedure for each station is as follows:

–Station 1 (Location: Pitcher's mound and backstop)
Athletes stand to the right of the mound and take turns hitting fungos into the backstop. A player stays near the backstop.

Each player receives four swings. He must hit two single-bouncers into the backstop and two double-bouncers into the backstop. Have players record and average the number of successful hits on a scoring card (Card 1).

STATION 1: SCORING CARD

STATION 1				
Player	Single-Bouncer	Double-Bouncer	Avg. Successful Hits	Points

–Station 2 (Location: Second base)

A player goes to deep center field and stands near a glove. The remaining players stay next to second base. An athlete, with one foot resting on second base, fungos a ball to the glove. He hits the ball twice. After he hits the ball a second time the distance between the ball and glove is measured with a measuring tape and recorded on a scoring card (Card 2). When all players have hit, they repeat the same procedure and fungo to the second-base bag. Measurements are recorded on the card.

STATION 2: SCORING CARD

STATION 2				
Player	Distance to Glove	Distance to Base	Avg. Distance	Points

–Station 3 (Location: Right field fence or sideline fence)

Stand a tire against the fence. Athletes remain about 90 feet away from the tire. A player stands near the tire, acting as judge. Each athlete makes five throws at the tire. A player earns 5 points for hitting the inside of the tire and 2 points for hitting the outside wall. Scores are recorded on a card (Card 3).

STATION 3: SCORING CARD

STATION 3							
Player	Throw 1	Throw 2	Throw 3	Throw 4	Throw 5	Avg. Points	Points

Give athletes these rules for each station:

- Station 1
  - –An athlete must hit from behind the pitcher's mound. Penalty: 1 point.
- Station 2
  - –If a player misses or fouls the ball, he receives a score of 150 feet.
  - –If a player fails to step on second base, he comes in last.
- Station 3
  - –Do not allow players to take practice throws. Give them time to warm up prior to the drill.
  - –A player cannot take more than two steps forward. Penalty: 1 point.
  - –A player must use a three-quarter or overhand throw. Penalty: 1 point.
  - –If a player steps over the throwing line, his throw doesn't count.

Comments: See Comments, Drill 78, Four Stations.

INCLEMENT WEATHER ACTIVITIES

Here are three indoor activities for team athletes during inclement weather.

80 WIN OR LOSE

Objective: To practice hitting, fielding, and throwing.
Location: Gymnasium.
Technique: Players concentrate on meeting the pitched ball squarely in front of home plate, fielding cleanly, and making accurate throws.

Procedure: Have athletes do the following—

- Divide players into four groups, four per group. Send each group to a different quarter of the gymnasium.
- Give each group a different colored tennis or rubber ball. Each group consists of one fielder, one pitcher, and two batters. Use old rags or towels to mark left and right side foul lines. A movable rubber plate makes an excellent home base.
- The game begins when the players take the floor. Pitchers throw at one-half speed. CAUTION: Team pitchers should take special precautions not to strain their arms. Remind all players to throw the ball easily with a complete follow-through.
- The first hitter comes to the plate. Each batter encounters the same situation: Score is 3 to 2, the pitcher's favor; hitter's hypothetical team has bases loaded with two outs. The pitcher winds up and throws the ball. If the batter strikes out, he receives one loss. If he gets a hit, the game is tied. He stays at the plate. If he delivers another hit, his team wins and he records one win; the pitcher picks up the loss.
- The batter may tie the game but fail to bring in the winning run. When this happens, the pitcher receives one win; the hitter one loss. All ties go to the pitcher.
- Batters take turns hitting. Every player keeps count of his win–loss record.
- Whenever a player loses or wins three games everybody rotates. The number one batter becomes the fielder; the fielder goes to the mound; the pitcher switches to the number two hitter; the second hitter becomes number one.

- Only swings count. Runners cannot advance on walks or batters struck by the pitched ball.
- The first round ends when every player gets a chance to play all positions. Time dictates the number of rounds played.
- All players are responsible for their own scores. The champion is the player with the best win–loss record.
- If the pitcher or fielder misses a ground ball or drops a fly ball or line drive, runners advance one base. Runners advance only one base at a time.
- Hitters have the option of swinging away or bunting the ball. If the batter bunts the ball, it must roll past the pitcher in fair territory before it is scored as a hit.

Comments: If the gymnasium is not large enough to handle four groups, reduce group size to two or three.

81 DEAD CENTER

Objective: To place hit the ball up the middle of the diamond.
Location: Gymnasium.
Technique: Players concentrate on meeting the pitched ball squarely in front of home pate.

Procedure: Have athletes do the following—

- Divide players into three groups, five per group. Send each group to a different area of the gymnasium.
- Give each group a different colored tennis or rubber ball. Each group consists of one batter, one catcher, two fielders, and one pitcher. Use a movable rubber plate for home base.
- Tape a target, eight feet by four feet, several feet up the gym wall. Place home base 80 to 90 feet away and directly in front of the target.
- The pitcher stands about 40 feet away from home base; the catcher remains behind home plate. Catcher should wear a face mask.
- The two fielders flank the pitcher; one stays to the left; the other stands to the right. They field all batted balls which bounce off the wall.

- Play begins when the pitcher throws the ball to the batter. CAUTION: Warn pitchers to throw easily with a complete follow-through. Fast pitching may cause arm strain. The batter receives three pitches. He concentrates on hitting the ball through or over the pitcher's mound.
- Players receive three swings, then rotate clockwise, e.g., catcher becomes hitter, hitter becomes left-side fielder, left-side fielder becomes pitcher, pitcher becomes right-side fielder, and right-side fielder goes behind the plate.
- Play "Wear Out the Middle," a point game. Award points as follows:

4 points	The batter hits a soft fly or line drive inside the taped boundary lines.
3 points	The batter hits a ball, either fly or line drive, which bounces once before striking inside the taped boundary lines.
2 points	The batter hits a ground ball which bounces several times before striking inside the taped boundary lines.
1 point	The batter hits a ball, either fly, line drive, or grounder, which strikes the taped area outside the target.
0 points	The batter hits a ball which fails to strike the taped borders or inside target area.

- The first player earning 16 points wins.

Comments: Players learn the value of concentration, a requirement for successful play. The coach should demonstrate the following points:

- A comfortable batting grip and stance
- How the choke grip helps a batter control his swing
- How the wrists, hips, and shoulders rotate in unison
- How to meet the ball squarely in front of home plate
- How to stride and follow through with the swing
- How a still head helps the batter keep his eyes on the pitched ball

Comments: Remind athletes to keep their eyes glued on the ball, swing easily, and follow through.

82 STAY ALERT

Objective: To let athletes practice defensive skills and coaching the bases.

Location: Gymnasium.

Technique: Players concentrate on fielding, throwing, running, and coaching the bases.

Procedure: Have athletes do the following—

- Set up a baseball diamond. Use movable rubber bases. Select two teams of infielders with six players per team.
- Play begins when the defense, Team A, takes the field. Team B, offense, comes to the plate without a bat. Two players (Team B) become base coaches. The coach holds a tennis or rubber ball and stands behind the catcher.
- The first man in line steps up to the plate. The pitcher simulates throwing a ball to the catcher. After a short delay the coach throws the ball onto the infield. The coach keeps the infield guessing by varying his tosses, such as ground balls, high bouncers, "nubbers", pop flies or line drives.
- After three outs, Team B takes the field; Team A comes to bat. Six outs constitute an inning. Different players coach the bases each inning. The coach determines the length of play. The team scoring the most runs wins.

Comments: Success comes only when both teams stay alert. A defensive man playing out of position or "cheating" toward a base may find the ball shooting past him. A line drive might catch a runner leading off too far.